The Daily Telegraph
Play Bridge at Home

Tony Forrester

B. T. Batsford Ltd, *London*

First published 1994

© Tony Forrester 1994

0 7134 7646 X

Typeset by Apsbridge Services Ltd, Nottingham.
Printed by Redwood Books, Trowbridge, Wiltshire
for the publishers,
B. T. Batsford Ltd, 4 Fitzhardinge Street,
London W1H 0AH

A BATSFORD BRIDGE BOOK
Series Editor: Tony Sowter

CONTENTS

INTRODUCTION

Both my father and mother were great bridge enthusiasts. Every Monday night the house would echo to sounds that seemed like a foreign language to me...

'He would be squeezed if he had the Jack of Diamonds.'

'Just lead a Club and play a loser on loser, then East would be end-played'.

'Take the Club finesse and throw North in.'

'Throw North in what?' I thought to myself.

My curiosity was fast getting the better of me, but I was told in no uncertain terms that I had to get my O-levels before I would be allowed to learn this mysterious game. I was eager to know what lay in store, having played cards at home from a very early age, but nevertheless this boy had to do what he did least well – be patient!

When the day came and my O-levels were out of the way, I sat down with my parents to be told the Facts of Bridge. From that moment to this, I have been totally hooked on the game, and I entirely understand why I had to complete at least part of my education before the game took charge.

I hope to engender that same enthusiasm in you, because bridge is the ultimate card game. Not only is it a great test of mental agility, but it requires many other qualities to compete successfully. Memory, logic, psychology, awareness and the ability to bluff are just some of these. Before you can develop those skills, however, you need to have a thorough grasp the basics of how to play.

This book, the first in a trilogy, aims to help you do just that, whilst the rest of the series is intended to build on this sound base.

Tony Forrester
1994

PART ONE

GETTING STARTED

1
THE BASICS

Introduction

Isn't it amazing how many films seem to have a conversation similar to this:

"Where is your mother, Joe?"

"This is her bridge afternoon at the Singletons" comes the reply.

Or, alternatively you will see 'mother' in the drawing room with three friends around a table issuing forth some strange language.

"Three Clubs."

"I say Double."

"Four Clubs."

"Four Hearts." etc. etc.

No doubt a thought flashed across your mind; how nice it would be to learn how to play the game. Well, you have taken a very big first step along the road to achieving that and by the end of this book, you will be there.

What will open up for you is not only a thoroughly absorbing pastime, hobby or even obsession, but also a social and entertaining game which will increase your circle of friends.

In this first chapter, we need to examine what is required to play bridge and what we are aiming to achieve. So let us start at the beginning....

Set Up

Although it would be over-simplifying matters to say that all you needed was a pack of cards, it would not be far from the truth.

To begin with, bridge is a game for four players, which cannot sensibly be played by any other number (although some variations can be managed with three). The players sit down at a (preferably) square table in the positions of the compass:

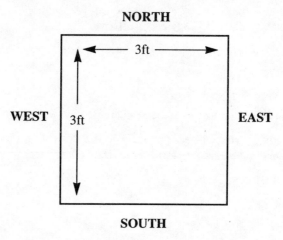

NORTH

SOUTH

In the above diagram, North and South will play together or be Partners, and will play against East and West. I will often refer to players as 'North, East, South and West' for ease of explanation, and you should always remember that North will be at the top of the page.

Now you have all sat down, we come to the pack of playing cards or, even better, two packs.

Cut for Partners and Preliminaries
The first step, unless it has been agreed in advance, is to settle the partnerships for the opening game or 'rubber', as it is called.

It is normal to spread a pack of cards (jokers removed), face down, across the table and each person draws one at random. The players with the two highest cards (Ace is always high in bridge, as you will soon see), play together, as of course do the two lowest.

The player with the highest card has two other responsibilities. He has the choice of where he sits (it is amazing how superstitious even hardened professional players are when it comes to that decision) and, should you have two packs of cards available, which one he will have for the first hand.

If, for simplicity, we call our packs 'red' and 'blue', then one partnership will always deal the red and the other side the blue.

Now we come to who shuffles and cuts, and this is achieved as follows:

> For the first hand of all, the 'highest card' will deal and the player to the left has the responsibility of shuffling.

> After the shuffle, this player should pass the cards over to partner (the player on the dealer's right) who will cut them, leaving the top half nearer to the dealer. The cut is then completed by the dealer who proceeds to distribute the cards one by one starting with the player on the left and following clockwise to each player in turn. The process should end with the last card being dealt to the dealer.

The next hand would be dealt by the player on the previous dealer's left and the mechanics rotate exactly as before. Note that, if using two packs of cards, the second deal will be with the other pack. It continues to alternate this way throughout that rubber.

Although this is how you should set up the table, it is not crucial to follow all these rules at first. All you *need* to remember are the following points:

> *Who plays with whom is determined by the cut.*
> *The first card is dealt to the player on dealer's left.*
> *The responsibility to deal a hand moves clockwise round the table.*
> *The positions are set for each 'rubber'.*

Here are three questions to recap the major points:

1. In a cut for partners, the players draw ♡Jack, ◇Queen, ♣4 and ♠King. Who plays with whom?
2. Who deals the first hand?
3. If South were dealing, who would deal the next hand?

The answers are:

1. ♠King plays with ◇Queen (and very nice for them too!)
2. The player cutting ♠King deals the opening hand.
3. West would deal the cards next.

Objectives

The first deal is now completed and all four players are about to pick up their cards (hands) and peruse them. Before you can get started, however, it is essential to know what you are trying to achieve.

Bridge is a competitive game where you and your partner (the person sitting opposite) are pitted against the other two players. Any whist players among you will quickly realise the fundamental importance of playing *with* someone rather than being on your own. An outstanding Bridge player is one who can successfully manage the problem of getting good results with a partner who may not be his ideal choice, or may not be at his best that evening.

Although there is much debate about who is the greatest player in the world, it is singularly irrelevant, because Bridge is all about partnerships and not an individual's performance.

Having established that we need to be 'half of a pair' to compete effectively, what is our partnership trying to achieve? There are two basic objectives:

1. By 'bidding' you will find out more about each other's cards and that process should determine what you 'contract' for. The more Aces, Kings and Queens you have, the higher your contract can be.

2. You attempt to maximise your score on each hand, either by bidding accurately or by defeating your opponents' contract. The more you can bid and still make, the more your reward will be.

So we compete against the other partnership at the table and on each hand we should aim to get a 'plus score'. That will be achieved by 'making the Contract', or 'defeating the opponents' Contract'.

Both 'Declarer Play' and 'Defence' are crucial in Bridge, as well as the ability to bid sensibly. In effect, there are three elements of the game and I will be covering each in turn.

In the meantime, though, we need to see how the basics of the game work by examining the rules.

2

RULES OF THE GAME

Bidding

After dealing the cards, we move onto the bidding. Before the play can commence, the 'Contract' needs to be established. In this section, I intend to deal with the mechanics of how we achieve that and how a sequence is constructed, starting with the first or 'opening' bid.

Once the deal has been completed, our four players should pick up their neat stacks of '13' in front of them and fan out the cards so they can see them all, but no one else can. The first person to act or bid – the 'first to speak' – is the player who dealt the hand.

This player has two choices – either to 'pass' or to make a positive call.

A positive call is any bid other than a 'Pass', and we must first understand what a positive call implies.

Bridge bidding is analogous to an auction. In the early days of the game, it was described as 'Auction Bridge' and even now the bidding sequence is frequently referred to as 'the Auction'.

North/South and East/West are competing against each other for the right to declare the contract and, by so doing, give themselves a chance of gaining points. Usually each side will try to find its best 'fit' i.e. the suit in which the total cards held by both players of a partnership is the greatest. So, for example, if North holds five spades and four hearts, and South holds two spades and five hearts, then the better fit will be in Hearts (nine cards) and not in spades (seven cards).

When one side has most of the strength or high cards (Aces, Kings, Queens and Jacks), but no fit, it can elect to play in 'No Trumps'. This means avoiding the problem of having no suit in which you have a pre-ponderance of cards, but still wish to declare a contract.

It is not possible to aim for fewer than seven tricks, the bidding starts from that base. So a minimum 'One Level' contract means you must win at least seven tricks to succeed, whereas a 'Two Level' contract would require eight tricks, and so on.

Level of contract	Minimum number of tricks required
1	7
2	8
3	9
4	10
5	11
6	12
7	13

A seven level contract, or 'Grand Slam' as it is known, requires one side to win all the tricks or fail. Hence, as you can imagine, such contracts are very rare and carry a great bonus should you succeed in bidding and making one of them. I had played several months before I dared to attempt a grand slam – and, worse still, I did not succeed. It will be a proud moment when you bid and make your first grand slam.

Anyway, we have established that a positive call implies an expectancy of winning more than half the tricks with that suit as trumps.

All four players have an opportunity to contest the auction and the mechanics are quite specific. Starting with the dealer, the bidding moves clockwise around the table, each player having one bid in turn. Hence, the order would be South, West, North, East if South had been the dealer of a given hand. If West had dealt, North would follow him and so on.

Each call or bid must be higher than the previous one, exactly as per an ordinary auction. Otherwise a player must say 'pass' when it is their turn. A higher bid can be defined in two ways. Either by a higher number, so two of any suit will always outbid one of any suit or second it can be in a higher ranking suit. Rank is a concept specific to Bridge and works as follows:

The highest rank is	No Trumps (NT)		followed by
2nd	Spades	(♠)	followed by
3rd	Hearts	(♡)	followed by
4th	Diamonds	(◇)	followed by
5th	Clubs	(♣)	

Spades and hearts are often called the Major suits (No, they do not vote Conservative) and we will see the reason why later, whereas clubs and diamonds are referred to as the Minors. Let's look at an example, so that you can see how the rank works in practice. Let us assume that South has dealt and opens 'one heart' (1♡). West is next to speak and needs to find a higher bid, or pass, i.e. the auction is already too high.

West could bid 'one spade' (1♠) or 'one no trump' (1NT) because they have a higher rank than hearts, but not 'one club (1♣) or 'one diamond' (1♦) because they are lower ranking. If effect, by bidding a minor you would be going backwards. To make a bid in clubs or diamonds, West must go to at least the next level up and select 'two clubs' (2♣) or 'two diamonds' (2♦).

Similarly, if South's partner, North, 'responds' to partner's opening, he too must raise the level. One can never go back in the auction. Hence the response must be 'one spade' (1♠) or higher. But, of course, the higher you go, the more tricks you are required to make.

How does the bidding end? Clearly, we cannot have an infinite process, there must be a way for the auction to close. The end is signified by three consecutive 'passes' or failures to make a positive call. The final contract will be the last positive bid prior to those three 'passes', so for example if the bidding develops as follows:

West	North	East	South
–	–	–	1♣
Pass	1♡	Pass	2♡
Pass	Pass	Pass	

The contract is 'two hearts' (2♡), declared by North/South.

Now just to make sure that everything is clear, try your hand at the following quiz:

Quiz on Bidding Rules

1. What is the lowest possible contract and what is the highest?

2. Who is 'first to speak'?

3. How many tricks do you need to succeed in a contract of 'three spades' (3♠)?

4. Who bids after East?

5. Which bids are not correct?

(a)
West	North	East	South
–	–	–	1◇
1♠	2◇	2♣	Pass
Pass	Pass		

(b)
West	North	East	South
–	–	–	Pass
Pass	1NT*	1♠	Pass
2♠	Pass	Pass	Pass

(c)
West	North	East	South
–	–	–	1♡
Pass	Pass	Pass	2◇
Pass	2♡	Pass	Pass
Pass			

* NT stands for 'no trumps'

Answers

1. 1♣ is the lowest; 7NT is the highest

2. The dealer of the cards

3. Nine (at least)

4. South

5. (a) East's 2♣ bid is lower than North's 2◇
   (b) East's 1♠ bid is lower than North's 1NT
   (c) There were three passes after South's 1♡ bid; that should have terminated the bidding.

Declarer and Dummy

We have seen how the auction is conducted and how it is brought to an end. As David Coleman would say "What happens next?". Bridge differs from all other card games in that one of the players, known as 'dummy', is about to place all their cards, *face up*, on the table. Dummy will be operated by 'declarer' who is dummy's partner. How do we establish who is declarer and who is dummy?

First we must go back to the bidding and see which side, North/South or East/West, are to declare the contract. This is easily done, because the last positive call, prior to the three passes which end the bidding, determines which side declares. So, in the following example, North/South declare the contract:

West	North	East	South
–	–	–	1◇
Pass	1♡	1♠	2◇
Pass	Pass	Pass	

The final bid is also the contract, so here North/South will play 2◇. To see who will play the hand, we need to examine who bid the trump suit *first*. Here with diamonds as trumps, South bid the suit first, so South is declarer and North becomes dummy. Let us examine another sequence:

West	North	East	South
–	–	–	1◇
Pass	1♡	1♠	2♡
Pass	Pass	Pass	

Again, North/South have made the last positive bid, i.e. 2♡, so their side will play the hand. This time, however, North has bid hearts *before* South, so becomes the declarer and South is dummy.

Opening Lead

When we have established who is to play the hand, the person on his left must find the opening lead. So when South is declarer, as per our first example sequence, West would begin the play. When North declares, the opening lead would be East's.

Once the lead has been made, *face up*, on the table, it is time for dummy to display his wares. Convention dictates that when the player who is to be dummy lays out his or her cards for all to see, the trump suit is always on the right (nearest to the leader) and other suits follow. A typical dummy in 2♠ would be presented as below (as viewed by declarer):

♠	♡	◇	♣
K	Q	J	J
J	10	7	8
6	4	3	4
	2		

Note the vertical arrangement of the cards so that all the players can easily see everything at a glance. With the same hand in a contract of 3◇, we might have the following layout:

◇	♠	♡	♣
J	K	Q	J
7	J	10	8
3	6	4	4
		2	

There are no rules governing the position of the other three, non-trump suits, but many people like to alternate red and black for ease of viewing and general artistry.

Declarer calls for, or selects, the card to be played from dummy on every trick. Dummy (*le mort* in France, recognising its very limited *rôle*) has no responsibility for any cards played during the hand. This makes being dummy one of the more boring bits of bridge. It is something akin to fielding at deep mid-on when Curtly Ambrose is bowling.

Nevertheless, the good news is that you are only dummy one hand in every four on average, and many players are grateful for the opportunity to rest and recharge their batteries.

So you are now at the stage where the opening lead has been made, dummy has 'gone down' and it is up to declarer to select which card to play. We are into our first bridge hand.

But just before we continue, try this **Quiz** to test your knowledge:

1.   Who is dummy?
2.   How is declarer established?
3.   How is dummy laid out?

Answers
1.   The partner of the declarer.
2.   The person who first bid the trump suit.
3.   With trumps on the right and in 'vertical' form.

Tricks

There are 13 tricks to be won or lost on all bridge hands. Each player must play a card on each trick so a competed or 'quitted' trick always contains four cards. The player who lays down the first card is the leader on that trick and we have already seen how the initial lead is established.

For the other twelve tricks, the lead is made by the player who won the previous trick. All the other players must follow suit, if they are able to do so. You are not allowed to keep a card back for later! As with the bidding, play is always in a clockwise direction and the highest card played, if everyone 'follows suit', will win the trick. So for example, if this is the layout of a given suit:

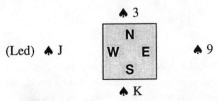

South wins the trick with the spade king, and would then decide what suit to play next. Remember, North and South are playing together, so avoid tricks like this one:

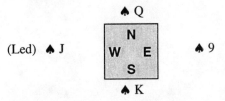

North has already won the trick with the spade queen, so there is no need whatsoever for South to 'win it' as well! They are partners and should play as such. There is no reward for coming first and second on any trick. It is a 'first past the post' system – no prizes for second place.

Sometimes you cannot follow suit as in the following example:

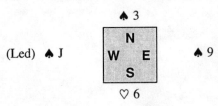

Playing as South, you have no more spades in your hand, so cannot follow suit any longer. You may choose *any* of your remaining cards to 'discard' on this trick, but would, as a matter of course 'ruff' if you possessed a trump (see next section). If hearts were not trumps in the example on page nineteen, West would have won the trick and would retain the lead.

Note, however, the power of leading.

Let's slightly adjust the example:

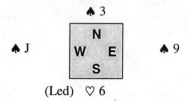

♠ 3

♠ J

♠ 9

(Led)   ♡ 6

Now, South has led ♡6 and the other three players, none of whom have any hearts left, all discard spades. If spades were not trumps, then South has won the trick and not West as in the previous example. It is important to remember that the rank of the card is only relevant when you are following suit. You can discard, as here, a card of greater rank than the one led, but still not win the trick.

A silly example would be:

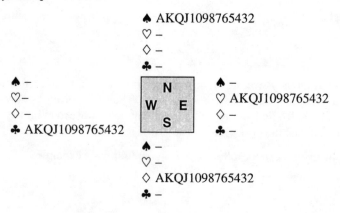

♠ AKQJ1098765432
♡ –
◇ –
♣ –

♠ –
♡ –
◇ –
♣ AKQJ1098765432

♠ –
♡ AKQJ1098765432
◇ –
♣ –

♠ –
♡ –
◇ AKQJ1098765432
♣ –

If there were no trumps, whoever led would win all thirteen tricks. If West led, the last trick would probably be:

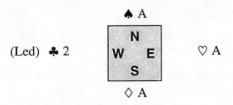

♠ A

(Led) ♣ 2

♡ A

◇ A

Unusual, to say the least, but West would still have won the trick.

Now for a brief **Quiz** to recap this section:

1. Who leads on the fifth trick?
2. When does a player make a discard?
3. When does playing a spade on a heart win the trick?

Answers
1. Whoever won the fourth trick.
2. When the player has no cards left in the suit led.
3. When it is a trump.

Trumps and No Trumps

I have alluded briefly to the concept of trumping or – 'ruffing' to give it the correct title – in the previous section, now is the time to expand on this. In the play of a hand, the most critical suit is 'trumps'. We have seen how we arrive at which suit is trumps. The end of the bidding also determines the side to defend and the player to declare the contract. But how does the trump suit affect the play?

Again, whist players will be familiar with trumps: any trump has more power than another card that is not a trump. For example:

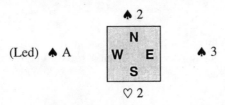

♠ 2

(Led) ♠ A

♠ 3

♡ 2

In the above diagram, hearts are trumps. South's ♡2 will win the trick despite the fact that West has led an ace. Sometimes the position can become more complicated:

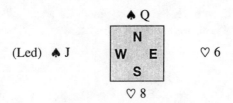

Hearts are trumps and spades are led, but neither East nor South has any spades left. When North beats West's lead, East trumps and if South had a spade it would be East's trick. South, also without spades, can 'over-ruff' East, thereby recapturing the trick for North/South. So the highest trump contributed to a given trick automatically wins it.

Hence, the ace of trumps is your only guaranteed winner, and is thus rightly regarded as the most valuable card in the pack.

Sometimes, the final contract is in 'no trumps' as per the example bidding below:

West	North	East	South
Pass	1♠	Pass	1NT
Pass	3NT	Pass	Pass
Pass			

South is the declarer, because, just as with suit contracts, the first mention of 'no trumps' predetermines who declares the hand. The contract is 'three no trumps' (3NT) by South. During the play, there will be no ruffing. If, for example, West has the lead and has the only two cards left in a suit, they will both win a trick. All that is needed is lead them and no-one can possibly beat either, however many aces, kings and queens they may hold in other suits.

It is a satisfying feeling to lead out a lowly *two* and find other players having to discard aces and kings.

Here is our usual **Quiz**, see how you get on:

1. Which card do you most want to hold?
2. If you 'trump' an opposition winner, what is the technique called?
3. What does 'NT' stand for?

Answers
1. The ace of trumps, the card that must win a trick.
2. Ruffing.
3. No trumps, where the ability to ruff is not available.

3
SCORING

Part-Scores, Games and Slams

Before we move on to the detail of bridge scoring, let me first outline the meaning of certain terminology that will come up repeatedly.

I must begin by saying there is little or no logic in how we arrive at our scores, and to some extent the apparent randomness causes more confusion than it is worth. Certainly it is sensible to play your early hands independent of any scoring table, so as to familiarise yourself with the basic concept, i.e. it is good to make contracts and bad to go down in them.

However, to progress to any level in the game, it is necessary to master the bridge scoring method and we start here.

There are four different types of contract, referred to as :

> Part-scores
> Games
> Small Slams
> Grand Slams

The contract is measured by the bidding and not by the number of tricks you make. So for example, if the auction is:

West	North	East	North
–	–	–	1♠
Pass	3♠	Pass	Pass
Pass			

The contract is 'three spades' (3♠), which requires at least nine tricks to succeed. You will not increase your score significantly by winning thirteen tricks as opposed to nine. If you happened to win thirteen tricks, you would not have achieved a 'Grand Slam', just 3♠ with four overtricks, as denoted below:

3♠ + 4

To maximise your score, you should have contracted for thirteen tricks by bidding to 'Seven Spades' (7♠), a Grand Slam. However, if only twelve tricks were made, then you would have gone down, resulting in a 'minus score', i.e.

$$7♠ - 1$$

You have to speculate to accumulate.

Here is a table showing the various levels you need to reach to collect certain bonuses:

Level	NT	♠	♡	◇	♣
One	PART-SCORES				
Two					
Three					
Four	GAMES				
Five					
Six	SMALL SLAMS				
Seven	GRAND SLAMS				

The chart shows how a given contract is described, and is relatively easy to follow for the higher contract levels. Bid and make a seven-level contract (thirteen tricks) and you have a grand slam, whereas the six-level (twelve tricks) is a (small) slam.

Where bridge scoring gets rather difficult is in the area of 'game', where you must reach different levels according to the 'suit' chosen.

In no trumps, the three-level (or nine tricks) will suffice, whereas in spades and hearts (the majors) ten tricks are needed. If that were not confusing enough, in diamonds and clubs (the minors) you need eleven tricks.

Failure to reach these lofty heights will result in you achieving a part-score, so-called because it is part-way to scoring a game.

I said earlier that the higher you go, the greater the reward, otherwise there would be no advantage to ever venturing above the one-level. Let us look next at a scoring chart, and see how many points you get for your efforts:

In the minors, you score 20 points per level, in the majors this is raised to 30 points per level, and finally in no trumps, it is 40 points for the one-level and then 30 for each additional trick . Are you lost?

Level	NT	Suit ♠ ♡		◊ ♣
One	40	30		20
Two	70	60		40
Three	100	90		60
Four	130	120		80
Five	160	150		100
Six	190	180		120
Seven	220	210		140

If you are trying to find the logical thread holding this together, as you probably will be, don't! Just remember these tables for now and keep them open on the table when you begin play, until you become familiar with their contents.

In addition to the simple points for tricks taken, you also achieve bonuses for reaching game and beyond. I will move onto these in the next section.

Here is a short **quiz** to check you are up-to-date.

1. What are the following contracts? Part-score, game, slam or grand slam:

    (a) Three Spades
    (b) Three No Trumps
    (c) Four Clubs
    (d) Six Diamonds
    (e) Five Hearts

2. How many tricks are needed to make game in Diamonds?

3. If you bid 'Four Spades' and make 12 tricks, what type of contract have you made?

Answers

1. (a) Part-score
    (b) Game
    (c) Part-score
    (d) Slam
    (e) Game

2. Eleven

3. A game (with two 'overtricks').

Rubbers

Bridge at home is 'Rubber Bridge', as opposed to 'Duplicate Bridge' which is prevalent at club and tournament level. Rubber bridge has a unique scoring method based on two premises:

1. The level of contract bid and made.
2. Above and below the line scores.

To understand more easily what is involved, we must look at a standard score-sheet:

WE	THEY

It is normal practice to enter scores for your side in the WE column and losses under THEY. It is advisable, as an aside, for all four players to keep the score, particularly in your early games. The advantages are twofold:

1. It helps to ensure the scoring is accurate and understood by everyone.
2. The current 'state of play' which can affect tactics is known to everyone (I will cover this area in greater depth later in the Series).

Winning the Rubber

Each rubber will have an eventual winner and loser and this will be determined by the first side to achieve 100 points *below* the line, twice. They will win the rubber on the second occasion 100 points or more are scored.

However, as stated in the last section, you score points below the line according to the level of the contract you reach, as opposed to the number of tricks won. This apparent inconsistency works in the following way.

You and I bid 3♠ and make ten tricks, this is scored as:

WE	THEY
30	
90	

Below the line, i.e. the critical area of scoring, we achieved three spades (the contract) or 90 (see chart earlier). Our overtrick (worth 30 points) goes above the line. However, had we bid to four spades and made the same ten tricks, the result would be:

WE	THEY
120	

We would collect our first 'game' or half-way towards the rubber, because we have (at least) 100 points below the line. We should draw a line under that score, as it is safely in the bank.

In effect, we have scored the first goal or won the opening set.

The battle to see who will secure the next game now commences - a rubber is in effect the 'best of three games'.

A side that has won one game, as we have here, is said to be 'vulnerable'. From that point to the end of the rubber, the penalties for failing to make contracts (undertricks) will be doubled (see section that follows) and the bonuses for making slams will be increased.

If our opponents now make game, it is 'game all' and everyone is vulnerable. This situation is often the most cut-throat in bridge, as each partnership strives to get the all-important third and decisive game. It is akin to the final set of a tennis match, where pressure can play a part in the eventual outcome, and good nerves are needed to be successful.

However, if we manage to repeat the result of 'four spades making' on the second hand, we would have won a very easy (and fairly unusual) rubber in just two deals. We would then get our 'rubber' bonus points which are:

1. An additional 700 points if we win the rubber by two games to nil; or
2. An additional 500 points if we win by two games to one.

Thus in our easy, mythical rubber, our final score is:

WE	THEY
700	
120	
120	
940	

We have won by 940 points (or a nine point rubber).

Rubber bridge scores are normally recorded in round 100's. Scores ending in from 10 to 50 are rounded down to the hundred below and scores ending in the range of 60 to 90 are rounded up to the whole hundred above.

The need to score 100 points or more below the line is the reason that lies behind a different number of tricks being required to make game depending on the suit played, i.e.

No Trumps   1 x 40 + 2 x 30 = 100 – hence *three no trump* is enough
Majors   4 x 30   = 120 – hence *four of a major* and
Minors   5 x 20   = 100 – hence the *five level* is required

How do the pair, who reached 3 ♠ and made an overtrick, fit into the scheme of things? They have a 90 partscore, so they need any other score below the line, i.e. *any* contract made, to top them up to the magical 100 and record their first game.

If they are allowed to play the following hand in 'one heart', and achieve seven (or more tricks), they will have converted their partscore into a game. The score sheet would look like this:

WE	THEY
	30
	90
	30

There is one potentially nasty thing that can happen to that part-score, however. It could be wiped out at a stroke if you secure a game before they have a chance to convert it.

If, for example, the second hand (after the initial 3♠ contract) results in you making a game, 3NT for the sake of argument, then our score-sheet would look like this:

WE	THEY
100	90

A line is drawn below the 100 for 3NT, and the effect of the part-score as a stepping-stone to a game, is lost. As soon as game has been achieved, everyone begins again from zero. You can begin to see much of the advantage that is gained from a game contract as opposed to a part-score. In tennis terms, in one instance you have won the set, whilst in the other you are serving to win it.

I will break there for a moment to ask some questions:

Quiz

1. You bid to two spades (2♠) and make eleven tricks, how many points do you score below and above the line?

2. How many points do you need to make a game?

3. You make two clubs with an over-trick on the first hand of a rubber and one no trump on the second. Have you converted your partscore into a game?

4. How many games do you need to win a rubber?

5. What is the bonus for winning a rubber?

6. What is the fewest hands required to win a rubber?

Answers

1. 60 below and 90 above.

2. 100 points (or more)

3. No. Two clubs with an overtrick scores 40 points below (and 20 points above) as does 1NT. You only have 80 points so far below the line.

4. Two.

5. 700 points if your opponents have not made game, 500 points if they have.

6. Two.

Scores above the Line

So far I have concentrated almost exclusively on scoring below the line, because that is what will ultimately win you a rubber. However, we must not dismiss scores above the line, because they count equally when adding up the final result.

Above the line scoring can be achieved by any of the following:

1. Overtricks
2. Bonuses for Small and Grand Slams
3. Honours
4. Bonuses for doubled and re-doubled contracts
5. Penalties for undertricks

I will cover each in turn.

Overtricks

Overtricks are scored at their trick value (see chart on page 25) – 30 for no trumps and the majors or 20 for the minors. We saw how this worked in the previous section. If we play in four hearts and make an overtrick, it is customary to put '150' below the line because it is game, rather than 120 below and 30 above, but this is only shorthand and in no other way different.

A good rubber will not have too many overtricks as they often represent a failure to bid high enough. The corollary will be seen shortly under 'penalties for undertricks'.

Bonuses for Small and Grand Slams

If we take thirteen tricks in hearts, we have seen that the basic score is 210 (7 x 30 for each trick over six). If we have reached game i.e. four or five hearts, then we have 120 points below the line or game, and that is our bonus. If however we have bid up to the six or seven level, we score an additional bonus above the line as follows:

	Non-Vulnerable	Vulnerable
Small Slam (six)	500	750
Grand Slam (seven)	1000	1500

The grand slam bonus is twice that for the small slam. Note the increased figures when you are vulnerable i.e. you have one game already. A side that bid a game on the first hand and followed with a slam on the second would have a score sheet looking something like this:

WE	THEY
700 (ii) 750 (i)	
100	
180	

(i)   Bonus for making the slam on the second hand
(ii) Rubber bonus (2-0)

That would add up to 1730 points or a 17 point rubber. Ouch! An average rubber is in the region of 5 to 7 points, so anything in double figures represents a healthy victory.

Honours

'Honours' are a quaint, old-fashioned aspect of bridge which for some unaccountable reason have not died away with the passage of time. Two things must occur for an honour bonus to apply:

1. They must be held in the trump suit.
2. They must be held in the one player's hand (whether declaring, dummy or even defending).

If these two statements hold good, then for possessing four of the A, K, Q, J and 10 you score 100 points and all five gets you 150 points.

In no trumps you need all four aces in one hand to score 150 points, otherwise there is no reward. Personally, I feel it is adding insult to injury to not only have to play against someone holding all these important cards, but to be penalised as well. However, like it or not, that is the rule.

Before moving on to our last two methods of scoring above the line, a brief re-cap:

1. If you bid and make a grand slam on the first hand of a rubber, what is the bonus?
2. If you score two overtricks in a club contract, how many points are entered above the line?
3. You play four hearts and dummy has ♡AKJ102. Do you have an honour bonus and if so, how much?

Answers
1. 750 points.
2. 40 points.
3. Yes, 100 points.

Bonus for doubled and re-doubled contracts
I have not, as yet, mentioned the process by which we could arrive in a doubled or re-doubled contract and that will be dealt with later in the series. For now, I will simply say that the action of 'doubling' an opponent expresses the view that he will not make his contract and re-doubling suggests that the doubler is wrong!

Doubling and re-doubling increase both the bonuses for making a contract, and the penalties for failing to do so. The system is as follows:

1. The below-the-line trick score is doubled (or re-doubled). So two diamonds doubled making would accumulate 80 (2 x 40) points. If re-doubled it would be 160 points, and the result would mirror a game contract.

2. Doubled overtricks are automatically 100 points non-vulnerable and 200 points vulnerable. Re-doubled ones are 200 and 400 respectively.

3. There is a constant bonus of 50 points above the line often referred to as '50 for the insult' (of being doubled in a contract that makes). In effect your opponents have insulted your bidding without due course, and must pay for it! If redoubled this bonus is increased to 100 points.

To test your scoring prowess, try these examples – first non-vulnerable and then vulnerable:

1. Two clubs, doubled with one overtrick.
2. One No-Trump, redoubled, just making.
3. Three Spades, doubled with two overtricks.

Answers
Non-Vulnerable

1.   80 below and 150 above.
2.   160 below and 100 above.
3.   180 below and 250 above.

Vulnerable
1.   80 below and 250 above
2.   160 below and 100 above (as non-vulnerable)
3.   180 below and 450 above

Penalties for Undertricks

Until now, the focus of the book has been fairly and squarely on making contracts. I have only mentioned, in passing, that a contract may be defeated or 'go down'.

Sometimes, even the most apparently simple contract may be defeated by bad distribution of the cards, and our more speculative ventures in search of a great reward, are always liable to suffer a sad fate.

When we say we will make something in the bidding and we fail, we have to pay a price. The price is higher if we fail by many tricks or we are doubled or we are vulnerable. The table below should explain the process:

Contract	Non-Vulnerable			Vulnerable		
number of tricks down	Undoubled	Doubled	Redouble	Undoubled	Doubled	Redouble
1	50	100	200	100	200	400
2	100	300	600	200	500	1000
3	150	500	1000	300	800	1600
4	200	800	1600	400	1100	2200
5 etc	50 for each extra trick	300 for each extra trick	600 for each extra trick	100 for each extra trick	300 for each extra trick	600 for each extra trick

As you can see, the effect of 'doubling' is not just to double the penalty if a contract is not fulfilled; with larger penalties the results are more dramatic. Hence, it is always an important part of bridge to judge when to double and when not to. It is quite feasible to find a situation where your opponents win the rubber (by eventually making two games), but you win the money!

Re-doubled contracts are rare indeed, but are very exciting because of the huge number of points at stake.

Your final test at bridge scoring is:

1. If you bid 3♢ and fail by two tricks, how many points do you concede?

2. You double vulnerable opponents in 4♣, and it fails by three tricks, how many points do you score?

3. You play 4♠, non-vulnerable, and make only six tricks, what do you concede?

Answers
1. 100 points, non vulnerable and 200 points if vulnerable.
2. 800.
3. 200 points (4 x 50).

That concludes the section on bridge scoring and I am sure that at this stage you feel that you will never master it. Please don't be put off. You will soon come to terms with the 'regular' scores that happen frequently, and that is really all you need to know.

Even current international players are not sure what some contracts score without hasty reference to a scoring table or a pencil and paper.

The two main things to bear in mind are:

1. A rubber is won by scoring two game contracts. This is achieved by twice reaching 100 points below the line.

2. Below-the-line scores can only be achieved by making contracts.

Finally, here are two mythical rubbers to score. See how you get on.

Rubber One

Hand One	WE play in 2♠, making ten tricks.
Hand Two	THEY play in 5♣, making eleven tricks.
Hand Three	THEY play in 4♣, doubled making seven tricks.
Hand Four	WE play in 3♠, making nine tricks.
Hand Five	THEY play in 4♠, making thirteen tricks.

Complete the scoresheet. Who 'pays' who and how much?

Rubber Two

Hand One	WE play in 6♠, making thirteen tricks.
Hand Two	WE play in 4♠, making seven tricks.
Hand Three	THEY play in 2◇ doubled, making nine tricks.
Hand Four	THEY play in 1NT, making eight tricks.
Hand Five	WE play in 4♠, making eight tricks.
Hand Six	WE play in 3NT, making eleven tricks.

As before, complete the scoresheet and calculate the result.

Rubber One

Your scoresheet should look like this:

WE	THEY
800 (3)	700
60 (1)	90 (5)
60 (1)	100 (2)
90 (4)	120 (5)
Total Points **1010**	**1010**

It is a tied rubber. Even though you 'lost' two games to zero, your double of 4♣ earned enough to tie the score.

Rubber Two

WE	THEY
500	200 (5)
60 (6)	30 (4)
500 (1)	150 (3)
30 (1)	300 (2)
180 (1)	
	80 (3)
	40 (4)
100 (6)	
Total Points 1370	800

We won by 570 points, or a 6-point rubber. That was achieved primarily by successfully bidding and making a small slam on the first board.

A good short-cut to being confident with the scoring is to make up a rubber of your own and see how it translates into scores.

Now it is time to move on and I next want to look at 'Your First Game'.

PART TWO

YOUR FIRST GAME

4
BIDDING AND PLAY

Bidding

Let us analyse a bridge auction and see how it was constructed:

Dealer South. Love All.

West	North	East	South
–	–	–	1♡
Pass	1♠	2♣	2♠
3♣	3♠	Pass	Pass
Pass			

The four players, North, East, South and West are about to commence a rubber. The first hand is dealt by South, having cut the highest card when selecting partnerships. As it is the first hand, the score is 'Love All' – no-one is vulnerable.

South considers his or her hand and deems it to be worth an opening bid of 1♡. In Part Three, we shall see how this decision was arrived at, but for now let us proceed with the bidding.

West decides not to enter the auction at a higher level than the opening bid, so has no choice but to pass. North, with a spade suit to mention, 'responds' to partner. A response should confirm the presence of a suit and some high cards. However, North is not raising the level, so a strong hand is not necessary. East is prepared to enter the auction, holding a club suit and a fair share of aces, kings and queens. East 'competes' or 'contests' the bidding by 'overcalling' 2♣, believing that despite North/South's apparent strength, a club contract is possible.

It is quite conceivable that, on a given hand, both sides can make a sizeable number of tricks in a trump suit of their own choice. Hence, we get competitive bidding where the thrust and parry of bridge is at its height.

South has spades with North and is not prepared to allow East to steal the contract, so bids 'two spades' (2♠). North/South have found a fit, and South has suggested that they shouldn't try for more than eight tricks. With a better hand, South could have bid three or even four spades.

West comes to life, and supports partner's club suit. Although too weak to come into the bidding to start with, West can perform a subsidiary role, and also make life difficult for his opponents.

North has a choice of actions. He might bid game, 'Four Spades' (4♠) with a good hand, make a competitive bid of 'Three Spades' (3♠) as here, or 'Pass' with a weak hand. Alternatively, if East/West look as if they have over-reached themselves, North could 'double' the contract of 3♣ and try to score a healthy result 'above the line'.

After North's 3♠ bid, all the players feel that they have had their say, and are happy with the contract. North will play the hand and will need to make nine tricks to succeed.

I will now show you the actual layout of the four hands, and you can decide for yourself what actions you might have taken during the bidding and whether you feel the final contract is satisfactory.

Dealer South. Love All.

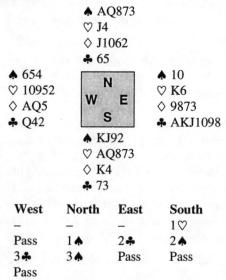

```
                    ♠ AQ873
                    ♡ J4
                    ◇ J1062
                    ♣ 65
    ♠ 654                          ♠ 10
    ♡ 10952          N             ♡ K6
    ◇ AQ5         W     E          ◇ 9873
    ♣ Q42            S             ♣ AKJ1098
                    ♠ KJ92
                    ♡ AQ873
                    ◇ K4
                    ♣ 73
```

West	North	East	South
–	–	–	1♡
Pass	1♠	2♣	2♠
3♣	3♠	Pass	Pass
Pass			

Final Contract: 3♠, to be played by North

Please note the 'bridge diagram' above. It is the normal way to represent how the fifty-two cards are laid out. We can see at a glance all the players' hands, the dealer, the vulnerability and the bidding below.

I will be using this type of diagram again later, so take a moment to familiarise yourself with it.

Many bidding sequences are not competitive and just involve one partnership attempting to find it optimum contract, for example:

Dealer South. Love All.

West	North	East	South
–	–	–	1 ♡
Pass	1 ♠	Pass	2 ♠
Pass	4 ♠	Pass	Pass
Pass			

Here, East/West have nothing to say and it is North/South who do all the bidding. Most auctions start at the 'one-level' as here and progress towards the final contract, often in a slow-slow-quick way. 'Slow' whilst a fit is being established and quick when one has been.

This sequence has reached game because North has decided that the extra bonus gained by getting a game contract is worth the risk of failing to make enough tricks. Note how, even though they have nothing to say, East and West always have to bid at their turn. Sometimes one can lurk in the undergrowth during the early rounds of the bidding, only to come out with a bid later. On this hand, they must content themselves with trying to win at least four tricks and defeat North's 4 ♠ contract.

If they succeed, they will have gained a plus score despite holding the weaker hands at the table. You could be unkind and say that they have profited from North/South's greed. What is fairer to say, is that North/South over-reached themselves in search of the bonus they would get for a game contract.

Play

Let us remain with our first example hand and see how the play starts. We already know that East will make the opening lead when North plays the contract.

After East has made his selection, South will 'table his dummy'. North should then assess the chances of success, based upon the knowledge of all his side's assets.

It is in these early stages of the play where declarer's advantage is at its greatest. For declarer will be able to tackle the appropriate suit, will have no problem knowing what partner's cards are, and, even more important-ly, will know whether the contract is under threat from weakness in a given area or if it is relatively safe.

The defence has no such comfort. This difference tends to make playing the hand as declarer an enjoyable and thoroughly entertaining experience, whereas defending is often very hard work indeed. Nevertheless, there is much pleasure to be gained from accurate defending, especially if both players have combined well to defeat an apparently impregnable contract. Partners in defence must help each other and I will be looking at ways in which they can 'signal'. In effect signals can enable one to look through the backs of the cards and into partner's hand.

Also, the very weakness of a defender's situation, i.e. the uncertainty of the location of crucial cards, can also, ironically, be one of the strengths. Often the success or failure of a particular contract will hinge on the posi-tion of a specific card: for example, the queen of trumps is regularly the bane of declarer's life. It is the defence's task to keep to themselves which one of them possesses that key card and not to let declarer find out easily.

A couple of general do's and don'ts.
For declarer: if there is a route to making the contract without taking risks, you should always follow it. Never concern yourself about extra (over) tricks as they will bear little impact on your success as a rubber bridge player in the long term.

For defenders: if you can see a sure way to beat a contract, do it. Again, worrying about undertricks is not the way to win at rubber bridge. Make sure that you beat contracts whenever possible, rather than always trying to beat them by the maximum possible.

In my own experience, there have been many greedy players who sought to maximise their result on every hand. Very few were winning ones.

Finally, it is crucial that all players keep their emotions to themselves during the bidding and play. It is not part of bridge to show your appreciation of, for example, your partner's lead by grinning broadly across the table. Like poker players, bridge players need to remain as expressionless as possible during the play of the hand.

This need starts at the beginning when declarer greets his dummy. A show of discontentment will only alert your opponents to the fact that all is not rosy in the garden. You have given something away. That is allowed, it just isn't very sensible.

It is allowed primarily because your partner, i.e. dummy, cannot benefit from the information, whereas, if you were defending and looked upset at any card played by your partner, you would be transmitting information which he might then use. Partner should not use your conduct as a guide, but it is much better that you do not give him the chance.

If I have seemed to dwell on this matter of table ethics, or etiquette let me assure you of two facts:

1. What I am preaching is hard to follow, because it is human nature to react sometimes, even when one should not. Particularly so when you know your partner has just done something which has adversely affected *you*.

2. Table manners are critical in bridge. Without them, the game would descend into chaos very quickly. Do your best to preserve the image of the game. In the end it is more rewarding to work something out for yourself, rather than being 'told' by the expression on partner's face!

Having said all that, bridge is a truly social and highly pleasurable pastime and much amiable banter is quite permissible at the table *between* hands. You will soon distinguish between that and displeasure shown at cards played during the hand.

Tricks

How do we keep track of the tricks won and lost during the play and what happens to cards already played? The answers to both questions are linked.

Assume for the moment that these are the cards played on the first trick:

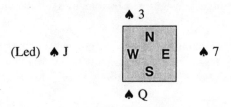

South is declarer (we know this because West had the opening lead) and has won the first trick with ♠Q. South will then collect the four cards played and lay them face downwards in front of him.

He then leads to trick 2. Let us assume that South also wins that trick. The process of gathering the cards is repeated, but instead of simply 'stacking' the two tricks, they should be placed alongside or at right angles to each other, for example:

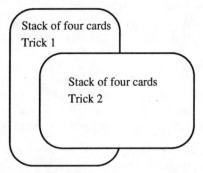

In this way the task of determining tricks won to date is significantly easier than it might otherwise be.

If one of East or West (the defenders) wins a trick they decide which of them, usually the first to obtain the lead, will keep the stacks of cards. Any player can check the numbers of tricks won by both sides at any time, but it is impolite to do this when your partner (if defending) is about to play. For example, it may be taken as a reminder that only one more trick is required to defeat the contract, so he had better play his ace now!

A trick that has been gathered in is called 'quitted' and can be viewed up to the time that either player of that side plays to the following trick. Thereafter it is dead.

When play has ceased on a hand, both sides should know the result. However, if any doubt exists, a quick reference to the tricks taken should settle any dispute. If these are poorly arranged, it may prove necessary to add up all the cards held by each side and divide them by four to determine the tricks won. Finally, all should become clear.

It is time for the next deal to commence and time for you to move onto your first bridge lesson!

Before that, our usual re-cap:

1. How do you describe the vulnerability on the first hand of a rubber?

2. What does 'contesting' the bidding mean?

3. How does one 'support' one's partner?

4. What is an uncontested auction?

5. When is dummy 'tabled'?

6. When is it acceptable to show displeasure?

7. What happens to cards already played?

Answers
1. 'Love All' or no-one vulnerable

2. When both sides, North/South and East/West are bidding against each other on the same deal.

3. By bidding his suit at a higher level (also called 'raising partners suit')

4. One which only North/South or East/West bid, but not both.

5. After the opening lead has been placed on the table.

6. Never!

7. They are stacked in front of the side that won them as tricks (face down).

5
WINNING TRICKS

Top Tricks

To date I have concentrated on bidding and how the final contract is arrived at. Before I move onto specific sections on bidding, declarer play and defence, it is important to establish our final basic rule. How do you win tricks?

The easiest way to win tricks is to 'cash' aces and follow with kings and queens etc. However, very few contracts can be successfully managed in so-called 'top' or 'quick' tricks. Let us look at one:

Dealer South. Love All.

♠ A42
♡ AQJ7
♢ A42
♣ 953

♠ K53
♡ K4
♢ KQ7
♣ KQJ106

Contract: 3NT by South. Opening Lead: ♠J

The declarer, South, has arrived in 3NT ('three no trumps') and needs to acquire nine tricks in some manner. The first task, as soon as the opening lead has been made, is to assess top tricks.

A top trick is one that can be taken straight away, without the need to lose or risk losing the lead. If you are playing as South what are your top tricks? Add them up for yourself.

In spades, you have the A and K   = 2
In hearts, you have the A, K, Q and J   = 4
In diamonds you have the A, K and Q   = 3
In clubs you have none (the ace is missing) = 0
Total = 9

South is lucky: this is a contract that requires nothing more than to take the top tricks in a sensible order. The only suit where care may be needed is in hearts. Let us look at that suit in isolation.

♡ AQJ7

♡ K4

Four tricks need to be taken and it is good technique to start with the honours held in the shorter suit. There is no requirement to begin with the Ace. So first play ♡K from South and ♡7 from North, then with the lead still held by South, play ♡4 to dummy's ♡J.

North can then cash ♡A-Q and we have negotiated the suit. If we begin by taking one of North's tricks first, say ♡A, South will be left with ♡K alone, (singleton). When we play the second round, we will be stuck!

♡ QJ7

♡ K

The king will win the trick, but the ♡QJ (despite being winners) may be marooned. The lead is in the wrong place at the wrong time. If we had accidentally, whilst thinking of something completely different, played the suit in this manner, we would need an 'entry' back to the North hand, in order to cash the queen and jack of hearts.

In other words, we would need to arrange for the lead to be in the North hand, and that, as we have seen earlier, can only be organised by North winning the previous trick. Our 'entry' to North would be via the card which won that trick.

On our example hand, North has two such immediate entries, ♠ A and
♦ A, so even if you mis-managed the heart suit, help would be easily to
hand. Sometimes, you are not so lucky:

Dealer South. Love All.

♠ 963
♡ AQJ7
♦ 963
♣ 963

♠ A42
♡ K3
♦ AK42
♣ AK75

Contract: 3NT by South. Opening Lead: ♠ J

Again, you arrive in 3NT on a spade lead and start by assessing your top
tricks:

In spades, you have the A	=	1
In hearts, you have the A, K, Q and J	=	4
In diamonds, you have the A and K	=	2
In clubs, you have the A and K	=	2
Total	=	**9**

Lo and behold, nine tricks are available in top tricks – another easy game
to make. However, if you are careless in the heart suit and fail to cash
South's ♡ K first, the resultant 'blockage' will lead to your defeat. Two of
your top tricks will have disappeared, leaving only seven.

The top tricks available in a given suit nearly always total the number of consecutive honours held, starting with the ace and working downwards. So:

A42

K63

represents two tricks, whereas:

A42

KQ3

represents three. However, you cannot have more top tricks than the length of the longest suit in either your hand or dummy, so all these combinations:

AJ   A42   AKJ   AK

KQ4   KQJ   Q4   QJ4

despite holding AKQ and J, are still only three top tricks. Extending the suit length concept, how many top tricks do we have in this suit?

A642

KQJ85

We have the top four honours between the hands and a four card suit or longer. Therefore we have at least four top tricks. However, South has five cards in the suit: does this mean we can add a fifth trick, or not?

To answer this question, we need to consider the entire layout of the suit. First, we total up the cards held between our two hands; 5 + 4 = 9. That leaves four (13-9) for the opposition. If one player held all the four cards outstanding, he would follow suit on the ace, king, queen and jack, but then he would have no cards left in the suit.

Our last card in the South hand would automatically be a winner because it would be the last card outstanding (the thirteenth) in the suit. Hence, we can add an extra trick and call this suit five 'quick tricks'.

What about:

A64

KQJ85

Again, you have all the honours and a five card suit for South, but North has only three cards now. Do you have four or five top tricks?

Using the same logic as before, the opposition has five cards, which could all be in one hand. In that case, one opponent would be able to beat the last card in the South hand. Technically, we have only four 'toppies'.

However, it is extremely unlikely that either of our opponents will have been dealt all the outstanding cards and, therefore, our holding approximates more closely to five top tricks than to four. We would be very unlucky indeed if we assumed, and based our strategy upon, five tricks being available in this suit, and found only four.

As we delve more deeply into card play, the statistical or percentage side of the game will become more evident. A mastery of odds is essential for top class bridge, but would not be expected at home. It is true, however, that the more comfortable one is with percentages and odds, the easier bridge card play becomes.

Let me pause there to re-cap 'top tricks':

1. How do we define a 'top' or 'quick' trick?
2. Dummy has ♠AKJ7; you have ♠Q4, Which honour should be cashed first?.
3. What is an entry?
4. Consider the following combinations. How many top tricks are there in each case?

A73	QJ98	KQ	K
N	N	N	N
S	S	S	S
KJ106	A43	AJ	AQJ1043

Answers

1. A trick that can be taken without losing the lead.

2. ♠Q, otherwise the suit will be 'blocked'.

3. A winner in the hand opposite to the one currently holding the lead.

4. **(a)** Two (Ace and King).
   (b) One (Ace).
   (c) Two (The length of the longest suit!).
   (d) Six (Unless one opponent holds all six outstanding cards.)

Establishing Tricks

In the previous section we saw how to calculate our top tricks. When we have enough of those we can simply 'cash out' or take them immediately and claim our contract.

However, few contracts can be made in this way – otherwise bridge would give us as much mental stimulation as a game of Snap! The vast majority of hands require other techniques to establish tricks.

Dealer South. Love All

♠ A42
♡ AJ76
◇ A42
♣ 953

♠ K53
♡ K4
◇ KQ7
♣ KQJ106

Contract: 3NT by South. Opening Lead: ♠J

If the hand seems familiar, it is the one on page 49, with ♡Q removed from dummy and replaced with ♡6.

On the spade lead, our first task, as always, is to assess our top tricks:

In spades, we have the A and K	= 2
In hearts, we have the A and K	= 2
In diamonds, we have the A, K and Q	= 3
In clubs, we do not have the A	= 0
Total	**= 7**

We could 'cash out' the first seven tricks but, as we need nine, that would be two short. When our winners were exhausted, the opponents would take the remaining tricks. We must attempt to find those extra two tricks from somewhere. Again, we should first look at each suit in turn and consider their possibilities for development:

(a) Spades

After taking the ace and king, the opposition have all the remaining honours and more cards in the suit than we have (seven to six). No prospects here.

(b) Hearts

After the ace and king have been cashed, the queen might fall promoting our jack. Alternatively, we could 'finesse' (see next section) the jack, but this would only gain one further trick. We still need more.

(c) Diamonds

When we have taken the ace, king and queen we will have no diamonds left to establish!

(d) Clubs

If we play a club honour (say ♣K) it will be beaten by the opposition's ace. However, now ♣Q will be the highest card, etc., etc. In effect, we can promote or establish several tricks in clubs.

♣ 953

♣ KQJ106

So our approach to 3NT should be: win the opening lead and continue with ♣K to drive out the ace. We lose that trick. However, on re-capturing the lead, we have top tricks in clubs, because ♣Q has become the highest outstanding card. We create four club tricks in total which when added to our top tricks in the other suits, gives us eleven. We comfortably make our 3NT contract, with two overtricks.

How do we calculate the number of tricks that we can establish in a given suit? First to be able to set up tricks with certainty, we require a 'sequence' of cards, e.g. KQJ or QJ10, but they do not have to be held in one hand. These two combined suit holdings are identical for trick establishment purposes:

QJ109   Q1074

| N |
| S |

| N |
| S |

764   J96

Both are missing the ace and king, but are 'solid' thereafter. Thus we can use the queen and jack to drive out the opposition's top cards and then we will have the ten and nine to cash. Eventually, despite missing the top two cards in the suit, we will have developed two tricks ourselves.

If we have at least four consecutive cards in a suit, the number of tricks we establish is simply the length of our longest suit minus the number of top cards missing. Here are a few examples:

(a) Q107

| N |
| S |

J9642

Longest suit	=	5
Top cards missing	=	2
Tricks to establish	=	**3**

(b) KQ4

| N |
| S |

J1073

Longest suit	=	4
Top cards missing	=	1
Tricks to establish	=	**3**

(c) Q74

| N |
| S |

J109

Longest suit	=	3
Top cards missing	=	2
Tricks to establish	=	**1**

(d) J93

| N |
| S |

1084

Longest suit	=	3
Top cards missing	=	3
Tricks to establish	=	**0**

Note that, when the longest suit is only three cards, we only require three consecutive 'honours', so these suits are effectively the same.

Q74

J109   J102

Both generate one trick – eventually!

Here is an example hand to help us analyse the optimum approach to establishing tricks:

Dealer South. Love All.

♠ K74
♡ QJ7
◇ J107
♣ KQJ7

♠ AQ3
♡ 10962
◇ Q98
♣ A104

Contract: 3NT by South. Opening Lead: ♠J.

Our usual scenario of South playing a contract of 3NT. Let us see how you should be thinking about the hand (try to formulate your plan before reading on).

As always, you start with the addition of your top tricks in the hope that they will equal nine and you can have an easy time. Here you have seven (three in spades, four in clubs), two more are needed from hearts and diamonds.

Next you look at those two suits in isolation to see which one is the better prospect.

Hearts should provide you with four (longest suit in South) minus two (missing the ace and king), i.e. two tricks. Diamonds produce only one extra trick (because the longest suit is only three cards). You have the answer – play on hearts straightaway.

A word of caution on the way to tackle any suit where we have different lengths in dummy and declarer's hand. Look at these examples:

(a) QJ7   **(b)** KJ104   **(c)** J1082

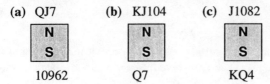

10962   Q7   KQ4

Each holding is perfect for us to develop tricks, i.e. four consecutive honours, but we must be careful to play the suit in the correct manner. Just as we saw earlier in the example when we had top tricks, *we must play the honours from the shorter suit first*, to avoid a 'blockage' occurring.

If in (c) we began with the jack, losing to the ace, the balance of the suit would look like this:

1082

KQ

That situation is at best messy and at worse catastrophic when dummy has no entry to its 'long trick'.

Before I move on to other ways of developing tricks, a brief test:

1.   When do we need to establish tricks?

2.   How many tricks will I win with these combined holdings?

(a) KJ7   **(b)** J10842   **(c)** QJ

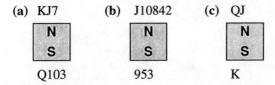

Q103   953   K

3.   To be sure of establishing tricks, how many consecutive honours are needed?

Answers

1. When our top tricks do not add up to the tricks required to make the contract.

2. (a) Two   (b) Two   (c) One.

3. Four. However, three will suffice if the longest suit in either hand is only three cards (e.g. 2(a) above where the 'ten' is unnecessary).

The Finesse

The finesse is probably the most commonly used technique to create tricks out of thin air. The basic idea can be illustrated by the following example:

AQ

64

As declarer, you require two tricks in this suit. With the ace and king it would be easy, but here we are missing the king. Also we cannot establish any tricks, because we do not have any consecutive honours to promote later. We appear to be stuck.

However, there is a way to give us a chance of making two tricks exactly half the time.

As a general technique, it is usually best to lead 'towards' honours that are not in a sequence, rather than lead away from them or lead them out. In this example, you have the following ways to play this suit:

1. Lead from North, queen first.
2. Lead from North, ace first.
3. Lead from South and play the ace, follow with the queen.
4. Lead from South and play the queen, follow with the ace.

Which do you think has the best chance of gaining the all-important extra trick?

1. Lead the queen from North.
    The opponents will take the queen with their king and leave you the ace for later. One trick with no additional chance.

2. Lead the ace from North.
    The king may appear, thus promoting the queen, but the opponents have nine cards in the suit, so the chance of a player having a singleton king is remote indeed. A tiny extra chance.

3. Lead from South, play the ace.
    Exactly the same as 2. The only time this will succeed is when the king falls under the ace.

4. Lead from South, play the queen.
    As you will now have guessed, this is our best chance for success.

Consider these two layouts of the suit:

(a)

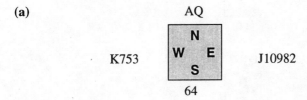

(b)

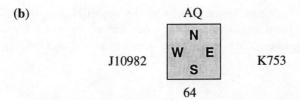

In (a) above, when you lead from South and West follows, you play the queen. Can East beat the queen? The answer is 'no' because the king is in the West hand. East could lean across the table and grab it, but that would be a trifle obvious! No, East has to follow with a small card and the queen has become a trick.

In (b), however, East does indeed have the much-sought-after king, so can win the queen when North plays it. Now the ace is North/South's only winner.

So, half of the time, i.e. when the king is in the West hand, our ace, queen combination wins two tricks and half the time it only wins one.

This makes determining exactly how many tricks you will win in a given contract extremely difficult. It is our first brush with percentages and odds. It will not be the last, because mastery of this aspect of the game is crucial to winning bridge. A contract which depends upon a finesse for its success is 50%. When it succeeds you score heavily, when it fails you lose points. Deciding if the gamble of bidding a dicey contract is worthwhile requires good judgement and a bit of luck.

Here are some other finesse positions for you to consider:

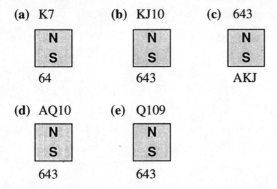

(a) K7   (b) KJ10   (c) 643

        N   N   N
        S   S   S

        64   643   AKJ

(d) AQ10   (e) Q109

        N   N
        S   S

       643   643

Let us examine each in turn and see how the finesse works.

(a) You must not lead from North. If you do, the king will lose to the ace and you will have promoted nothing. You can never win a trick. However, play from South first and you have a chance if the layout is:

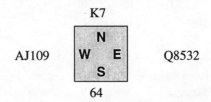

                        K7

                        N
        AJ109   W   E   Q8532
                        S

                        64

If West plays his ace, you play the seven from dummy and the king is now a trick. If West plays low, you put up the king and will win the trick because East cannot beat it. Switch East and West round and you can only ever win one trick.

(b) Again, you must get into the habit of routinely leading towards 'broken sequences' of honours like the one in the North hand. So start from the South hand. Let us look at how the suit may be laid out:

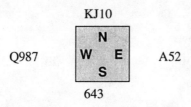

KJ10

Q987   A52

643

When you lead a low card, West follows with the seven. Do you play the ten or the king? If you try the ten and West has the queen, the only card that East can beat the ten with is the ace. Now you must be careful to continue correctly. After this play, you retain the following cards:

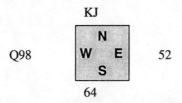

KJ

Q98   52

64

You could cash the king, but then the jack would lose to the queen. What you must do is lead from South again, this time putting in the jack from dummy. As you already know that West has the queen, the jack will win the trick. You have repeated the finesse and secured two tricks from the suit.

The second position is similar to starting with AQ because once the ace is dislodged, the KJ are promoted.

(c) An easy suit for experienced finessers like you, but remember that you must play towards the honours, so lead first from the North hand this time. This is what we are hoping for:

643

1052   Q987

AKJ

When you lead from North, East follows with the seven and you play the jack. With the queen in the East hand, the jack will win and we now have three tricks. Note here that no further finesse is necessary, unlike (b) and that we can cash the ace and king immediately. Often this is called a 'simple finesse'.

(d) Here we have two finesses in one suit or a 'double finesse'.

Consider these layouts:

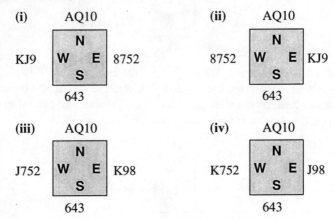

(i)	AQ10		(ii)	AQ10
KJ9		8752	8752	KJ9
	643			643

(iii)	AQ10		(iv)	AQ10
J752		K98	K752	J98
	643			643

Leading from South, you play low to North's ten. Why the ten, and not the queen? Well, the answer lies in layout (i). Here, if you first play the queen you will leave this position:

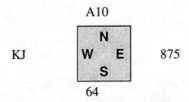

You win the ace, but not the ten which loses to West's king. If you first put on the ten, it will hold the trick because it's our lucky day - West has both the king *and* the jack (a 25% chance or 1 in 4). Now you return to the South hand via another suit and lead low to the queen in this position:

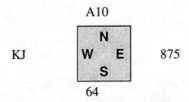

Sure enough, we have three tricks. How many tricks would we make in the other layouts? I'll leave that to you to work out.

What you should arrive at is one, two and two, which yet further compli-
cates our efforts to determine how many tricks we will win. Here, we are
faced with the following possibilities:

Number of tricks	% Chance
1	25%
2	50%
3	25%

Our average entitlement is two, or one of the king and jack in the West hand,
but we could make three on a good day, or one on a bad day. Suddenly,
the science of the game gives way to a little good old-fashioned luck!

(e) On our final example, we are missing both the ace and king of the
suit, so is this a finesse at all? Here is our hoped for layout:

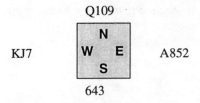

Q109

KJ7

A852

643

The finesse is against the jack (we can finesse against any card, but usually the ten is as low as we ever realistically need). When you lead towards
dummy, you intend to play the nine, and providing that the jack is in
West's hand, we will eventually win one trick. If East has the jack, we
will have struggled to no avail.

We have not finished with the finesse, however, because to date all the
examples have had the honours in one suit and small cards in the other. It
is possible to finesse in another way.

When you have a sequence of honours (this time only two are required)
you may be able to 'surround' a missing honour in an opposing hand.

Here is the principle:

A2

QJ

You need two tricks from this suit, how do you go about it?

If you cash your ace first, the king is most unlikely to appear, so you will finish up with one trick. If you play from the South hand and lead the queen, West holding the king, will have two unenviable choices:

1. Play a low card which will be followed by North's two. East will be unable to beat the queen because West has the king. The queen wins a trick, making two tricks in the suit; or

2. 'Cover' the queen with the king, i.e. play the king on the queen. Now we win with North's ace, and our lowly jack in the South hand is the highest card outstanding in the suit. We win two tricks again.

If East has the king in the example, we can only win one trick, so once more we have a 50% chance of a second winner.

Note how the jack is required to make the finesse work.

A2

Q3

When you lead the queen, all West need do is play his king. Now after winning the ace, you would be left with the two and three. Little prospect of a trick from them, I'm afraid. You win only one trick, regardless of the location of the king.

Before we move on, here are some suit combinations to try out for yourselves:

1. How should you tackle the following?

(a) A753   (b) A62   (c) J1084

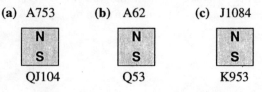

QJ104   Q53   K953

(d) AJ10   **(e)** KJ10

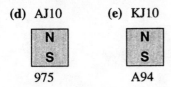

975   A94

2. What is your expectation of tricks won in each of the above examples?

3. In this suit:

KJ4

753

How many tricks could you expect to win and how often?

Answers

1. **(a)** Lead the queen, play low from North unless West plays the king. If the queen holds the tricks, play the jack and repeat the process. Then play the ace on the third round.

   (b) Lead the ace and then low to the queen. Do not lead the queen first, as it will be covered by the king and wasted. If this is the suit layout, however:

the Queen will score a trick by playing in the recommended way.

   (c) Lead the jack. If it loses to West's ace, return to North and lead the ten, repeating the finesse as often as is necessary. If the jack loses to West's queen, the suit will be solid, so simply drive out the ace and take the balance of tricks (2).

   (d) Lead low to the ten. If it loses to the king or queen, return to South and lead to the jack. We hope to find something akin to this:

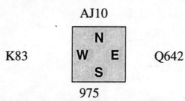

AJ10

K83   Q642

975

East will win the first round with the queen, but cannot then beat dummy's jack on the second round, when you finesse again.

(e) Take your choice! You can cash either the king or ace first and then finesse against either opponent.

(i)   KJ10   (ii)   KJ10

862   Q753   Q753   862

A94   A94

In (i) you need to cash the king and play the jack, playing low in South unless East covers with the queen.

In (ii) you need to cash the ace and play low to North's jack. How can you know which way to play? All will be revealed later in the series! For now it is enough to know you have a choice.

2.   **Frequency**   **Expected Tricks**

(a) 4 tricks   - 50%
    3 tricks   - 50%   or 3.5 tricks on average

(b) 2 tricks   - 50%
    1 tricks   - 50%   or 1.5 tricks on average

(c) 3 tricks   - 50%
    2 tricks   - 50%   or 2.5 tricks on average

(d) 2 tricks   - 75%
    1 trick   - 25%   or 1.75 tricks on average
    You only take one trick when East has both the king and queen.

(e) Depends on how good a guesser you are!

3.   Two tricks when West has both ace and queen - 25%)
     One trick when West has one of ace or queen   - 50%)
     No tricks when West has neither   - 25%)
     Thus, the average expectancy is one trick.

That is enough about finesses for now, but we shall return later in the series to look at other aspects of this highly valuable and frequently used technique.

Long or Slow Tricks

Let me first say that a 'long' winner or trick is not one that takes ages to play! It is a phrase used to describe the winning of a trick with a small card, achieved solely due to possession of length in a suit.

Here is a simple example of the process:

543

AKQ2

We require four tricks in this suit. These is nothing to finesse, nor anything to establish, you can only lead South's ace, king, queen and see what happens.

What we must rely upon to obtain our extra winner, is that the two is a long trick, i.e. there are no more cards left in the suit when we come to use it. As the opponents have six cards between them (thirteen minus seven), and we can only take three top tricks, they must divide 3-3.

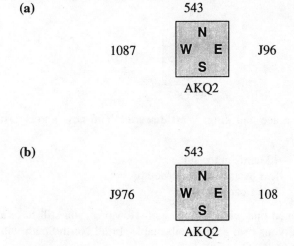

(a)

543

1087   J96

AKQ2

(b)

543

J976   108

AKQ2

In (a) we have what we need. The ace, king and queen will remove all the opposing cards leaving the two as the 'thirteenth' in the suit. A winner.

However, in (b), no joy. Here West has four cards, so he will retain the jack after three rounds of the suit. Our 'two' will be a loser – as indeed, it usually is.

The more cards you hold in a suit, the more likely you are to have long tricks:

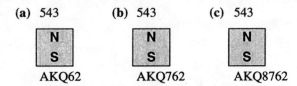

(a) 543   (b) 543   (c) 543

    AKQ62   AKQ762   AKQ8762

As our suit grows like Pinocchio's nose from four cards in the beginning to seven in example (c), our chances of success improve. In (a), the opponents now have only five cards between them, so it is less likely that any player will have four of them.

In (b), East/West have only four cards, so one player must hold them all to cause problems and in (c), they have only three cards. Thus in (c), you cannot be denied all your tricks (seven in total) because the opposition do not have enough cards to trouble us.

What do you do in (a) and (b) when the suit divides badly?

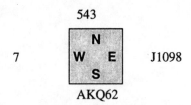

543

7   J1098

AKQ62

When you play the ace and king, West discards. You now know East started with four:

> 13 cards in the suit,
> less 8 cards in North/South,
> less 1 card for West

East cannot be denied one winner in the suit. However, you still have a long trick, because your fifth card is unbeatable. In all North/South will come to four tricks (A, K, Q and 2)

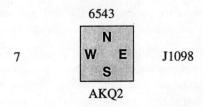

In this example, North/South have no long trick, as neither has a five card suit. Only three tricks will be won, as East will capture the fourth round of the suit.

Sometimes you do not need all the major honours:

If the opponents' five cards are divided 3-2 (which they are about two-thirds of the time), you will win the ace and two small cards in the suit.

Even a 4-1 division cannot prevent you securing one extra winner, although the 'result' in the suit will be 'opposition 3, home side 2', i.e. they win more tricks than you do.

Remember that to have any chance of establishing long tricks, one or other player must have at least a four card suit. Also, the combined holding must be a minimum of:

Longest Suit	Total Cards Needed
4	7
5	6
6	6

This is the ultimately feeble position that can generate an extra trick:

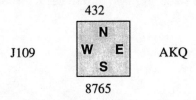

Eventually, if you have the patience, North/South will set up a winner in the South hand. It is rare to need to play on such a weak suit, but it can happen.

This brings the chapter on 'Winning Tricks' to a close. You have seen many combinations of cards and techniques to develop extra winners. If you are a bit overwhelmed at the moment, don't worry, because you will soon be at ease with playing cards once you get started. It is always less daunting to see things happening 'live' than it is to try and follow 'text-books'.

Before we move on to developing your bidding, a brief summary **quiz**.

1. (a) What is the shortest suit needed to establish a long trick?
    (b) Is there any other constraint?

2. If you hold ♠AKQJ2 in your hand, how many spades must come down in dummy to guarantee five tricks?

3. How many tricks would you expect to win with these suits:

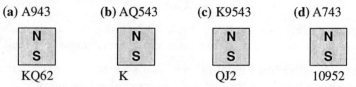

(a) A943	**(b)** AQ543	**(c)** K9543	**(d)** A743
N	N	N	N
S	S	S	S
KQ62	K	QJ2	10952

4. On the above hands, what is the fewest number of tricks which could be won?

Answers

1. (a) A four card suit.
    (b) Partner must hold at least three cards.

2. Four, then the opposition only have four Spades between them. Even if they are all in one hand, the top four cards will remove them, leaving the two as a winner.

3. (a) Four   (b) Four   (c) Four   (d) Two.

4. (a) Three   (b) Three   (c) Two (if East has A10876)   (d) One.

PART THREE

DEVELOPING YOUR BIDDING

6
THE OPENING BID

When to Open

I have talked quite extensively about the bidding sequence and 'how' one arrives at the final contract. Now is the time to see 'when' and 'what' you bid.

As you have already seen, the 'why' is to gain points by making contracts. Generally, the higher you go, the more you gain. However, to make contracts you need tricks, and to make tricks you need aces, kings and queens and some other good cards. Without some sort of method to establish just how many high cards your partnership holds, you might bid to too high a level, and find yourself playing a contract that is way beyond the combined assets of the partnership.

To avoid getting carried away, you must establish rules which will help you to assess the likely maximum level at which you can safely play. These rules are often called a 'system'.

A bidding system enables you to conduct a conversation with your partner, expressing meaningful information about your hand. Between the two of you, it should be possible to determine a final resting place, preferably one that doesn't turn out to be your funeral! The more information you can glean about partner's hand, the more accurate the final decision should be. Hence, longer bidding sequences, which reveal greater detail about what you hold, often prove necessary if you are aiming for a high level contract such as a game or perhaps even a slam.

When you arrive at a point where partner has conveyed enough information about their hand, it is time to bid the final contract.

The process begins with the decision whether to open the bidding or 'pass'. Even the lowest bid, 1♣, is an undertaking to win seven tricks (more than half), so it is logical that you need an above average hand to venture forth. How do you determine what is an 'above average' hand and what is not?

High Card Points

To assist you in that decision, you attribute points to your honour cards as follows:

$$
\begin{array}{rcl}
\text{Ace} & = & 4 \text{ points} \\
\text{King} & = & 3 \text{ points} \\
\text{Queen} & = & 2 \text{ points} \\
\text{Jack} & = & 1 \text{ point}
\end{array}
$$

There is nothing mystical or marvellous about these 'points', they are just an easy way, a shorthand, for describing the strength of a given hand. Here are some examples:

(a) ♠ AQJ6	(b) ♠ J10942	(c) ♠ A	(d) ♠ 7
♡ K10	♡ 6	♡ 97432	♡ KJ1073
◊ J942	◊ AK42	◊ AJ4	◊ AQ6
♣ AQ7	♣ J107	♣ Q1094	♣ A942

Add up the points yourself before reading on, as this is useful practice.

(a) has	2 aces	= 8	(b) has	1 ace	= 4
	1 king	= 3		1 king	= 3
	2 queens	= 4		1 jacks	= 2
	2 jacks	= 2			
Total points		**= 17**	**Total points**		**= 9**

(c) has	2 aces	= 8	(d) has	2 aces	= 8
	1 queen	= 2		1 king	= 3
	1 jack	= 1		1 queen	= 2
				11 jack	= 1
Total points		**= 11**	**Total points**		**= 14**

All very interesting, but how does it help?

An average hand is one ace, one king, one queen, one jack, one ten, one nine and so on. Adding up the points would give us 4+3+2+1 or 10 points (there are, therefore, 40 points in the pack).

To opening the bidding you need a better than average hand, thus an opening hand should have more than 10 points. Indeed, the generally accepted minimum requirement is 12 points.

The following are all minimum opening bids:

(a) ♠ J94	**(b)** ♠ 7	**(c)** ♠ Q6
♡ AQ7	♡ AQ97	♡ KQ10942
◇ AJ1092	◇ J974	◇ 753
♣ 63	♣ KQJ7	♣ KQ

All these hands have 12 points; just the requirements to open the bidding. With more points than this you would have a non-minimum opening, which would be expressed in your later bidding. For now, all you have said about your hand by opening the bidding is that you have at least 12 points.

Even that statement is capable of amplification, because not every 12 point hand is similar. I will discuss the impact of 'distribution' later, but for the moment let us assume that we measure the value of all hands by adding up their high card points.

Do you open on any of these hands?

(a) ♠ KJ109	**(b)** ♠ A654	**(c)** ♠ 7
♡ KQ10	♡ Q10972	♡ 64
◇ J987	◇ KJ	◇ AQJ1064
♣ J7	♣ K7	♣ KQ63

I would answer as follows:

(a) 11 points – **No**
(b) 13 points – **Yes**
(c) 12 points – **Yes**

What to Open

We have considered *when* you should open the bidding; the next question is *what* should you open?

The guiding principle is to begin with your longest suit and continue with the next longest, etc. So, if you have a six card suit, it is highly likely that you should open it. After all, by bidding you are proposing to win at least seven tricks with that suit as trumps. It makes sense, therefore, that you should choose your longest suit, to try and guarantee that you have more trumps than the opposition.

Now look at the six examples that follow and decide what you would open before reading on:

(a) ♠ A42
♡ Q9753
♢ AKJ2
♣ 8

(b) ♠ AQ6
♡ –
♢ AK98
♣ 1075432

(c) ♠ 5
♡ A109
♢ AK8764
♣ 983

(d) ♠ Q4
♡ KJ1094
♢ AQ985
♣ 6

(e) ♠ AJ94
♡ AJ94
♢ 4
♣ AJ94

(f) ♠ AJ4
♡ Q1072
♢ J98
♣ AQ4

(a)

      ♠ A42
      ♡ Q9753
      ◇ AKJ2
      ♣ 8

Recommended Bid: 1♡

Hand (a) appears to have two possible openings. In the 'red corner' you have a five card heart suit and in the 'blue corner' you have a strong four card diamond suit. Which packs the greater punch?

Remember, a basic principle of bridge bidding is that you always begin with your longest suit, regardless of whether the majority of your 'points' or high cards are contained there. This is a reflection of the fact that a trump is potentially more powerful than an ace, and hence your objective is to have as many trumps as possible.

Your partner, who has to co-operate in selecting trumps, needs to know which your longest suit is, before he or she can first assess the likelihood of that suit as the final denomination. If partner has 'support' i.e. four cards in your opening suit, you will have hit the nail on the head straight-away; if not, you will have to search for other possibilities.

So you open 1♡ and leave diamonds for the next round of bidding (see Chapter Eight).

(b)

      ♠ AQ6
      ♡ –
      ◇ AK98
      ♣ 1075432

Recommended Bid: 1♣

Hand (b) carries this principle even further. Here we have no points whatsoever in our longest suit, clubs, and yet we should still open 1♣ in preference to 1◇. Incidentally, I hope you have been mentally adding up the number of points in each hand. It is good practice and should help you become familiar with the 'point count' of a hand (this one has 13).

(c)   ♠ 5
                                   ♡ A109
                                   ◇ AK8764
                                   ♣ 983

Recommended Bid: 1◇

Hand (c) contains only 11 points and you will recall that previously I said that you needed 12 points to open. Do you pass then?

You could, and it would not necessarily be the wrong decision. However, this hand demonstrates that you need to look a little more deeply into the 'texture' of your cards before determining what to do.

You have a good six card diamond suit which represents considerable trick-taking potential. After all, the objective of the game is to take tricks. Look at this layout and will see what I mean.

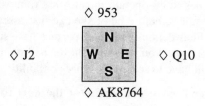

◇ 953

◇ J2   ◇ Q10

◇ AK8764

As South you are playing the contract in diamonds, and if this is how the suit divides you will win six tricks. When you cash the ace and king of the suit, East and West must follow suit which will leave them with no diamonds at all. Consequently, all the remaining small diamonds in South's hand will take tricks.

It is clear that you should recognise the additional strength of a long suit, so the rules for opening should be slightly amended as follows:

The minimum point-count for an opening bid is 12, *unless* you have a good six card suit (or longer) – in which case 11 points is acceptable.

(d)
        ♠ Q4
        ♡ KJ1094
        ◇ AQ985
        ♣ 6

Recommended Bid: 1♡

Now you face an inevitable question: what do you do when you have two suits of equal length? Well, you always knew it couldn't be as easy as just picking the longest suit, didn't you!?

Are there any firm rules or principles to apply here? The overriding one is 'economy of space'. Look at these two sequences, and you will see what I mean:

1.

West	North	East	South
–	–	–	1♡
Pass	1♠	Pass	2◇
Pass	2♡	Pass	Pass
Pass			

2.

West	North	East	South
–	–	–	1◇
Pass	1♠	Pass	2♡
Pass	3◇	Pass	Pass
Pass			

In each case, you hold (d) above. In the first sequence you open 1♡ (the higher ranking suit) and rebid diamonds thereby showing your two suits. Your partner, North, 'prefers' hearts to diamonds and, therefore, corrects the contract to 2♡. Note that your partner can choose either of your suits without going above the 'two level' (or eight tricks).

However, in the second sequence partner decides to select diamonds as the trump suit. However, this time, preference for diamonds takes you to the three level, forcing you to make an extra trick to succeed in your contract.

The second sequence is less economical than the first.

Hence, we should always open the higher ranking of two five card suits. I say 'always', but there is one exception.

Look at this hand:

♠ AJ942
♡ 7
♢ Q3
♣ AJ942

Again, we consider two likely sequences and see which one is more comfortable.

1.	West	North	East	South
	–	–	–	1♠
	Pass	2♢	Pass	3♣
	Pass	?		

2.	West	North	East	South
	–	–	–	1♣
	Pass	1♢	Pass	1♠
	Pass	?		

The first sequence fails to keep the bidding low – after all, you have a minimum opening so there is no reason to escalate your ambitions. The second auction though, is able to put across the message of your two suits and still remain at the one level, two tricks lower than the other approach.

So, in this one exception, it is better to open 1♣, the lower ranking suit, rather than 1♠. Otherwise, always pick the higher ranking suit.

(e)

♠ AJ94
♡ AJ94
♢ 4
♣ AJ94

Recommended Bid: 1♣

I suppose this hand is a Liberal Democrat's dream – a perfectly balanced three-cornered contest! Unfortunately, these 4-4-4-1 distributions, i.e. hands with three four card suits, can be a bridge player's nightmare. This is because you do not have enough cards anywhere to suggest strongly that they should be trumps. However, your partner may bid on the expectation that you have longer and more robust holdings in your suits and he may agree one of your suits as trumps – only to find that you have a minimal advantage, seven trumps to your opponents' six.

Nevertheless, this risk has to be accepted and you must choose your opening carefully to give your side the maximum chance of finding a 4-4 or better trump fit. The ideal scenario is that your partner 'responds' in one of your other suits and you will have found a fit straightaway. However, it is important that you keep the level as low as possible just in case no such fit exists, so always open your lowest four card suit and be 'economical'.

With example (e) you could open with a bid in any one of three suits. Let's consider what will happen if partner responds in your short suit:

1. You open 1♣.

West	North	East	South
–	–	–	1♣
Pass	1◊	Pass	1♡
Pass	?		

2. You open 1♡.

West	North	East	South
–	–	–	1♡
Pass	2◊	Pass	2♠
Pass	?		

3. You open 1♠.

West	North	East	South
–	–	–	1♠
Pass	2◊	Pass	2♡
Pass	?		

Sequence (1) has mentioned two of our suits at the one level and partner still has the chance to bid spades, which we will then 'raise'. Ten out of ten on economy grounds.

Sequence (2) has two inherent weaknesses:
   (a) partner had to respond at the two level;
   (b) a club bid will now take you even higher

Additionally, if partner prefers hearts to spades, he will have to climb to the three level to tell us.

Sequence (3) does not suffer from this last fault. However, the two points made above still hold good. In miles per gallon terms, (1) is a Metro, (2) is a Jaguar and (3) is a Granada.

(f)

♠ AJ4
♥ Q1072
♦ J98
♣ AQ4

I mentioned earlier that the absence of a five card suit in a hand suggests that there may be no advantage in seeking a trump contract. Then you cast your eyes in the direction of 'no trumps', and this example opens the doors for a discussion on no trump openings.

Before that thrilling instalment, a not so brief test:

Opening the Bidding Quiz

1. What are 'rules' in bidding often called?

2. How many points are there in a hand with two aces, two kings and two queens?

3. How many points are there in the following hands:

(a) ♠ AKJ107   (b) ♠ A   (c) ♠ 432
    ♥ AQ4   ♥ QJ73   ♥ J94
    ♦ J73   ♦ Q942   ♦ QJ107
    ♣ J4   ♣ AQ94   ♣ KQJ

4. (a) How many points do you need to open the bidding?
   (b) Are there any exceptions?

5. Which suit do you open?

6. With two or more four card suits, which do you open?

7. With two five card suits which do you open?

8. What is 'economy of space'?

Answers to Quiz on Opening the Bidding:

1. The 'rules' in bidding are often called a *system*.

2. 18. 8 for two aces, 6 for two kings and 4 for two queens.

3. How many points have the following:

(a) ♠ AKJ107	(b) ♠ A	(c) ♠ 432
♡ AQ4	♡ QJ73	♡ J94
◇ J73	◇ Q942	◇ QJ107
♣ J4	♣ AQ94	♣ KQJ
16 points	**15 points**	**10 points**

4. **(a)** You need at least 12 points to open the bidding.
   (b) The exception is 11 points with a good six card or longer suit.

5. You should open your longest suit.

6. With two or more four card suits, open the lower ranking.

7. With two five card suits open the higher ranking, unless you have clubs and spades.

8. 'Economy of space' is keeping the bidding as low as possible when describing your hand.

No Trump Bidding

Let me return to the sixth hand from the previous section:

♠ AJ4
♡ Q1072
◇ J98
♣ AQ4

I have only dealt with suit openings to date, but what about One No Trump? As you would expect for a bid suggesting that there is no trump suit, the opener should have no long suit to recommend. So a hand which has only one four card suit or even two with no singleton or void, is an ideal candidate for a no trump opening. So you should open 1NT with our example hand above or with a hand like:

♠ AQ42
♡ Q10
◇ J983
♣ A74

You open no trumps on what are often described as 'balanced' hands. This does not mean they are of sound mind and body – just that there is a balance of cards in each suit. You have seen the other, 'distributional', hands earlier, i.e. those with a five card or longer suit or in possession of a singleton or both.

Because an opening in no trumps describes the shape of a hand quite precisely, it is a valuable weapon. Partner can often judge immediately whether to play in a suit contract and which suit that should be, or in the absence of a long suit anywhere, that a no trump contract is best.

For example if your partner opens 1NT what would you do with these hands?

(a)	♠ J74	(b)	♠ AJ10942	(c)	♠ AJ10942
	♡ Q1094		♡ 7		♡ 7
	◇ KJ7		◇ J94		◇ AQJ
	♣ Q103		♣ Q106		♣ Q106

(a)

♠ J74
♡ Q1094
◊ KJ7
♣ Q103

Recommended Bid: Pass

With only 9 points and no long suit, you should simply pass and hope your partner can manage seven tricks.

(b)

♠ AJ10942
♡ 7
◊ J94
♣ Q106

Recommended Bid: 2♠

You can bid 2♠, confident in the knowledge your partner must have at least two cards in the suit. With just 8 points, the two level, a part-score, should be high enough. Try to convert it into a game on the next hand.

(c)

♠ AJ10942
♡ 7
◊ AQJ
♣ Q106

Recommended Bid: 4♠

On (c), you can also confidently bid spades, but here you have a hand which would have opened the bidding. It is important to remember the following maxim:

'An opening bid opposite an opening bid equals Game.'

This means that whenever your partner opens the bidding and you too hold an opening bid, then your combined hands should play a game contract and try for the game bonus. You won't always succeed, but it is worth the risk.

Here you are intending to play in spades and need to bid to the four level to reach game; so your answer should be 'four spades'. As your partner cannot have a singleton for his opening 1NT bid, you know that he has at least two cards in spades, giving you a minimum of eight between the two hands. That is our basic requirement for a trump contract.

Quiz on Opening 1NT

1. When do you open 'one no trump'?

2. What would you open with the following hands?

(a) ♠ AQ74   (b) ♠ KJ10   (c)♠ Q107
     ♡ 732   ♡ Q1094   ♡ A10
     ◇ 73   ◇ J98   ◇ Q9532
     ♣ AQJ5   ♣ AQ3   ♣ AJ9

3. How many points do you need to attempt a game contract when partner opens?

Answers

1. When you do not have longer than a four card suit and no singleton.

2. (a) 1NT or 1♣. Expert opinion would be divided between the two choices. Some would say that the hand is balanced and therefore 1NT is the most descriptive bid. Others would say that all the points are in two suits, and they would prefer to open 1♣ and re-bid 1♠. As you will often find in bridge everyone believes they are right!

    (b) 1NT. With the most balanced (and many believe the most boring) hand possible, allied to enough points to open the bidding the choice is easy.

    (c) 1NT or 1◇. Occasionally it is permissible to open 1NT even though you have a five card suit. The conditions that apply are:
        (i) the five card suit is very weak;
        (ii) you have honours in every suit.

    Again, opinions would vary as to the wisdom of either selection, the truth of the matter is that there is little to choose between the two. For now, let us stick to 1◇.

3. At least 12, because then we will have an opening bid ourselves. Regardless of whether partner is minimum or maximum, we would still wish to attempt at least a game contract.

That concludes the discussion of opening bids for now. I will return to the theme later in the series, when I will cover:

(a) Higher level openings and responses
(b) The range of 1NT openings and rebids.

7
THE RESPONSE

How to Respond to an Opening Bid

Your partner has opened the bidding, and is looking across the table expectantly, awaiting your response. How do you select your reply?

The rules are similar to those which determine the choice of your opening bid. You refer to the number of points you have and your longest suit.

Once you know that your partner has more than a fair share of points, as responder you should be able to see the likely potential of the combined cards. If you also have an opening bid, game should be available, but what if you have a weaker hand? Even when game values are assured, you still have to find your best trump fit, or decide to play in no trumps.

With the aid of a few examples I intend to show how the bidding should develop:

Your partner has opened 1♡, what do you respond on the following:

(a)	♠ AJ942	(b)	♠ J7	(c)	♠ Q75
	♡ Q93		♡ Q942		♡ 73
	◇ AQ4		◇ AQ42		◇ Q942
	♣ J7		♣ A73		♣ J842

(d)	♠ 73	(e)	♠ Q73	(f)	♠ QJ942
	♡ 72		♡ 73		♡ Q75
	◇ AQJ104		◇ Q1094		◇ J6
	♣ Q942		♣ A1094		♣ AJ4

Take a moment to form your view before reading on.

(a)   ♠ AJ942
                                          ♡ Q93
                                          ◊ AQ4
                                          ♣ J7

Recommended Bid: 1♠

As you have an opening bid, you are sure that you will eventually want to play in a game contract. However, your problems are not over. You still do not know which game to play in. Maybe partner's hearts are very good, suggesting 4♡ as a likely contract, or he may have reasonable spade support, leading to 4♠. Even 3NT may be the correct contract. How do you find out?

It is at this stage I have to introduce one of the corner-stones of effective bidding. When you open the bidding and your partner responds, *you must bid again*. This may seem strange at first, particularly as you may have only a minimum bid, but it is necessary because of the wide range of hands responder might hold. Often one bid cannot adequately describe a hand.

In effect this rule keeps the conversation alive, rather than trying to say everything in one sentence.

Bearing this in mind, you can safely begin with 1♠ on (a). Spades is your longest suit, and deserves a chance of being chosen as trumps. In any case, you can find out more about partner's hand from the next bid. Then you will find yourself in a better position to judge how to proceed.

(b)   ♠ J7
                                          ♡ Q942
                                          ◊ AQ42
                                          ♣ A73

Recommended Bid: 4♡

With this hand the question as to the choice of trump suit seems to have been answered. Partner has opened 1♡ and with four cards in hearts you have ample to support. With an opening bid, you can 'jump' to game straightaway by bidding 4♡. This type of call is often referred to as a 'limit' bid i.e. one where a player has limited his hand.

Once responder has chosen a limit bid, the obligation for opener to continue bidding is removed. After all, opener should be in a position to assess the combined maximum strength immediately.

Here are some other examples of limit bids in response to a 1♡ opening:

(i)	♠ A7	(ii)	♠ J1074	(iii)	♠ J6
	♡ Q943		♡ KQ73		♡ AQ1094
	◊ AJ7		◊ J107		◊ J94
	♣ 9842		♣ 42		♣ J73

(i) Bid 3♡. This achieves two things:

1. It shows partner support for his suit.
2. It suggests you can make nine tricks opposite a minimum opening bid.

It is then for opener to decide if there are any 'extras' that justify a game bid. Otherwise he just 'passes'.

(ii) Bid 2♡. This shows support, but not enough points to commit your side to the three level. Usually this limits you to about 6-9 points.

(iii) Bid 2♡ or 3♡. A hand typically in the middle where some players jump to 3♡ (maybe the ones whose partners play well) to suggest a game and others mournfully raise to 2♡. A marginal decision. With a better hand than this one you bid 3♡ (or higher), worse and 2♡ is enough.

All raises of partner's suit are 'limit' bids and I suggest the following scheme:

Raise to Two Level	=	6-9 points
Raise to Three Level	=	10-11 points
Raise to Game	=	12-15 points

With more than 15 points you should look for a slam, but we will leave slams to the next book! Remember to make game in a minor you have to bid to the five level and not the four level as here with hearts are trumps.

(c)   ♠ Q75
                                            ♡ 73
                                            ◊ Q942
                                            ◊ J842

Recommended Bid: Pass

Does responder always have to speak? As opener is forced to continue bidding, it is important that you do not reply on 'tram tickets'. The result would often be that the level of the auction rises beyond the ability to make a contract. You must tell partner immediately that you have a bad hand.

As a general rule anything below six points in responder's hand is not enough to bid. So here you pass 1♡. It is quite feasible that a better contract, e.g. 2♣, is available. However, the risk of getting well out of your depth in an attempt to find a better spot is too great. The time has come to hang up your boots.

(d)   ♠ 73
                                            ♡ 72
                                            ◊ AQJ104
                                            ♣ Q942

Recommended Bid: 2◊

This time you certainly have enough points to respond, but sadly there is nothing economical available, as bidding diamonds, your long suit, necessitates raising the level. That will require your side to make at least eight tricks and to make matters worse, your partner will bid again.

You are on a situation often faced in bridge, of having to choose from aless than ideal set of alternatives. We must bid 2◊, preparing to pass whatever partner does next. We will have gone as far as we wish to go!

(e)   ♠ Q73
                                              ♡ 73
                                              ◇ Q1094
                                              ♣ A1094

Recommended Bid: 1NT

Fewer points than (d), and you have lost your fifth diamond to boot. It is
not advisable to raise the level with a hand as weak as this, so your options
are significantly reduced.

You are left with a choice between 1♠ and 1NT. Clearly, 1♠ is out
because you do not have a spade suit, so that leaves 1NT. Without being
given a definition of what a 1NT response means, you have effectively
deduced it.

You reply 1NT to an opening bid if:

(i) You do not have enough points or a good enough suit to raise the
level (i.e. up to about 9 points or so).

(ii) You do not have a higher-ranking four card or longer suit (here the
only choice is spades, but, if partner opened 1◇, 1NT would rule out
four hearts and four spades).

(iii) You have the values to be worth a bid, i.e. 6 points or more.

Because your hand is this well-defined, a 1NT response is also a limit bid
i.e. the top range is limited by failure to bid at the two level. Hence, the
opener is not obliged to continue bidding. 1NT is 'not forcing'.

The concept of a forcing or non-forcing bid is one of the keys which
unlocks many doors. It has to be understood clearly to be able to bid sensibly. I will return to it more fully later in the series.

(f)   ♠ QJ942
                                  ♡ Q75
                                  ◊ J6
                                  ♣ AJ4

Recommended Bid: 1♠

Eleven points means that you are close to insisting on a game contract, but you do not have quite enough. Initially you have no problem, you can respond painlessly in your longest suit, spades, and see what happens. For example, if partner repeated his hearts, how would you proceed?

West	North	East	South
–	–	–	1♡
Pass	1♠	Pass	2♡
Pass	?		

It is too feeble to pass in case partner has a reasonable, above minimum, hand and a game is missed. However, you should not leap to game in case partner has a weak opening. You should solve this dilemma by making a 'game try'.

In this instance, you raise partner's hearts to the three level. By raising the level and yet still only being in a part-score, partner will realise that you must be suggesting higher things, but your raise does not force the opener to bid.

Thus South will bid 4♡ when he has an attractive hand and pass 3♡ if not. Of course, 3♡ may go down and then the decision to continue over 2♡ will have back-fired. Such is the nature of the beast. Bridge is all about calculated risk, and deciding when the potential gain justifies the possible loss.

Before we move on to how sequences develop further let me give you an extensive 'bidding challenge' to ensure that the principles of how to respond are fully understood:

Quiz on Responding

1. Your partner opens 1♣, what do you respond on?

(a)	♠ KJ73	(b)	♠ 7	(c)	♠ AQJ94	(d)	♠ Q8432
	♡ KJ73		♡ KJ92		♡ Q1072		♡ 973
	◇ 42		◇ J1073		◇ J		◇ Q107
	♣ 742		♣ QJ95		♣ A73		♣ 43

2. Your partner opens 1◇, what do you respond on?

(a)	♠ Q107	(b)	♠ J1082	(c)	♠ J1082	(d)	♠ Q108
	♡ J98		♡ Q7		♡ Q7		♡ J7
	◇ J7		◇ Q7		◇ Q7		◇ KJ953
	♣ K7532		♣ J9853		♣ AQJ94		♣ A94

3. Your partner opens 1♡, what do you respond on?

(a)	♠ K432	(b)	♠ AJ7	(c)	♠ AQ4	(d)	♠ AJ7
	♡ J7		♡ Q93		♡ 7		♡ Q93
	◇ 42		◇ J107		◇ AQJ10		◇ KJ5
	♣ J9853		♣ J984		♣ J9842		♣ Q984

4. Your partner opens 1♠, what do you respond on?

(a)	♠ 7	(b)	♠ 7	(c)	♠ 43	(d)	♠ 43
	♡ AJ942		♡ Q9852		♡ Q107		♡ Q109532
	◇ J942		◇ AJ1094		◇ Q1094		◇ J7
	♣ J94		♣ AQ		♣ Q1094		♣ J94

5. Your partner opens 1NT, what do you respond on?

(a)	♠ K9532	(b)	♠ Q107	(c)	♠ KQ10942	(d)	♠ KJ8
	♡ J		♡ Q3		♡ AJ4		♡ KJ94
	◇ Q1073		◇ QJ98		◇ K73		◇ Q107
	♣ J92		♣ KJ94		♣ 4		♣ Q94

Answers to Quiz on Responding

1. Your partner opens 1♣, what do you respond on?

(a)
♠ KJ73
♡ KJ73
◊ 42
♣ 742

Recommended Bid: 1♡

Remember about opening the lowest-ranking of two or more four card suits. The same principle applies when responding, except now it is slightly modified to the 'least space-consuming'. Here the two ideas coincide.

(b)
♠ 7
♡ KJ92
◊ J1073
♣ QJ95

Recommended Bid: 2♣

Always support partner immediately if you have four or more cards in the suit. Here you have eight points, so the two level is enough for now.

(c)
♠ AQJ94
♡ Q1072
◊ J
♣ A73

Recommended Bid: 1♠

As with openings, you begin with your longest suit, even if your points may be somewhere else. On this hand most of your points are in spades, so there is no problem. You intend to reach game, but that can wait, for now.

(d)
♠ Q8432
♡ 973
◊ Q107
♣ 43

Recommended Bid: Pass

Even though 1♠ may be a better contract than 1♣, you can never play there! This is because the opener must continue bidding (in case you had hand (c) for example). Hence any response is liable to raise the level of the contract with, in this case, little chance of success. It is best to pass and hope that partner can scramble home in 1♣ somehow.

2.   Your partner opens 1◇, what do you respond on?

(a)   ♠ Q107
                                         ♡ J98
                                         ◇ J7
                                         ♣ K7532

Recommended Bid: 1NT

You do not have enough points to raise the level (9 or more), so you cannot bid 2♣. Without a four card major to fall back on, you are left with a 1NT response.

(b)   ♠ J1082
                                         ♡ Q7
                                         ◇ Q7
                                         ♣ J9853

Recommended Bid: 1♠

You do not wish to respond at the two level on this poor collection, so your opportunity to mention the club suit is denied. It would certainly be reasonable to pass 1◇ but I feel that a response of 1♠ is just preferred. It is strange to find yourself showing a four card suit before a five card one, but the principle of keeping the level low on a weak hand is paramount.

(c)   ♠ J1082
                                         ♡ Q7
                                         ◇ Q7
                                         ♣ AQJ94

Recommended Bid: 2♣

Almost the same hand, but some 6 points stronger. The difficulties involved with responding at the two level have disappeared and you are free to start with your longest suit. You envisage continuing with the spade suit later, but you can consider that after you have heard partner's rebid.

(d)
♠ Q108
♡ J7
◇ KJ953
♣ A94

Recommended Bid: 3◇

A limit raise. In a minor, you often find that the need to take eleven tricks in game steers you towards other alternatives, 3NT or four of a major. Hence, opener with a fairly balanced hand and above minimum values will normally continue with 3NT which you would be delighted to pass.

3. Your partner opens 1♡, what do you respond on?

(a)
♠ K432
♡ J7
◇ 42
♣ J9853

Recommended Bid: 1♠

Exactly the same principle as 2(b) above. Note that you always bid 1♠ with a four card spade suit, in preference to 1NT. This is to enable a spade fit to be found when partner has a hand such as:

♠ AJ95
♡ AQ1084
◇ 63
♣ K6

(b)
♠ AJ7
♡ Q93
◇ J107
♣ J984

Recommended Bid: 2NT

With a balanced hand of 11 or occasionally 12 points and no good suit, you can respond at the two level in no trumps. Like 1NT, this is a limit bid, because with enough points for game, you would bid 3NT (see 3(d) below) directly. Hence opener can pass with a minimum hand (12 points) and raise to game with more.

(c)
    ♠ AQ4
    ♡ 7
    ◇ AQJ10
    ♣ J9842

Recommended Bid: 2♣

As for opening bids, if a choice of response exists, select your longest suit in preference to your strongest. Playing a trump contract is so much easier with longer trumps, not necessarily stronger ones.

(d)
    ♠ AJ7
    ♡ Q93
    ◇ KJ5
    ♣ Q984

Recommended Bid: 3NT

Following the example of (b) above, you prefer to show the nature and texture of your hand with a limit bid in no trumps. The alternative of 2♣ may lead partner to conclude that you have a better suit.

4.   Your partner opens 1♠, what do you respond on?

(a)
    ♠ 7
    ♡ AJ942
    ◇ J942
    ♣ J94

Recommended Bid: 1NT

Not enough to respond 2♡, so this is all we are left with.

(b)
    ♠ 7
    ♡ Q9852
    ◇ AJ1094
    ♣ AQ

Recommended Bid: 2♡

Again, note the similarity with how you open the bidding. The principle of 'economy of space' is crucial as the following two sequences demonstrate:

(i)	West	North	East	South
	–	–	–	1♠
	Pass	2♡	Pass	2♠
	Pass	3◊	Pass	?

(ii)	West	North	East	South
	–	–	–	1♠
	Pass	2◊	Pass	2♠
	Pass	3♡	Pass	?

In the first offering, South can easily show 'delayed support', for hearts and remain at the three level, whereas, in (ii), delayed support for diamonds would necessitate going to the four level. This would be bad for two reasons:

1. You would have gone past 3NT which may be your best game contract.

2. You have not found out about partner's heart support, making it difficult to arrive in 4♡ (the ten trick game). Your eggs are rather in one basket and not the right basket at that!

(c)
♠ 43
♡ Q107
◊ Q1094
♣ Q1094

Recommended Bid: 1NT

A simple problem for you now.

(d)
♠ 43
♡ Q109532
◊ J7
♣ J94

Recommended Bid: Pass

If you pass, how irritating it would be to find that partner had a four card heart suit *and* a good hand, for example:

♠ AK987
♡ AK87
◊ 6
♣ K107

Now there is an easy game available in hearts and we would be left floundering in 1♠. It happens. The odds are against finding such a hand are rather like backing a 100-1 outsider in the Derby – you do very well when it wins, but most times you'll lose your money. Better to pass and play the percentage game.

5. Your partner opens 1NT, what do you respond on?

(a)   ♠ K9532
                                      ♡ J
                                      ◇ Q1073
                                      ♣ J92

Recommended Bid: 2♠

If you allow partner to play 1NT, there is a distinct danger that the opponents will be able to win several heart tricks. The safer option is to 'correct' the contract to 2♠ and play in your suit. Partner, whose 1NT opening has described his hand, should pass.

(b)   ♠ Q107
                                      ♡ Q3
                                      ◇ QJ98
                                      ♣ KJ94

Recommended Bid: 2NT

Opposite a minimum opening of 12 points, game would not be available, but partner may have some extra strength. Give him or her the chance to bid game, whilst still leaving your side an excellent chance of a plus score even if the decision is 'pass'. A case of 'heads you win and tails they lose'.

(c)   ♠ KQ10942
                                      ♡ AJ4
                                      ◇ K73
                                      ♣ 4

Recommended Bid: 4♠

You have an opening bid and a good suit. You know that partner has at least two spades, so there is no danger of being short of trumps. It all adds up to game in spades.

(d)   ♠ KJ8
                           ♡ KJ94
                           ◇ Q107
                           ♣ Q94

Recommended Bid: 3NT

Here, you should be choosing between two and three no trumps. Although you have 12 points, it is a poor hand and one which you may have chosen to pass rather than open; your mental debate confirms this. My final selection reflects my faith in partner's ability to play the hand!

That concludes this section on Responses, but it is a subject that I will return to later in the series, when I will discuss amongst other things:

1. 'Jump' responses.

2. Responding to higher-level openings.

3. Conventional responses.

8
REBIDS BY OPENER

In the previous chapter, there were many sequences completed in one or two bids. Whilst they are the easiest to consider, they are only a fraction of all the possible auctions.

You need to develop a sound bidding theory because of:

1. The continuing search for a trump suit.

2. The accuracy required to reach successful higher-level contracts and to obtain the rewards that go with them.

As we have already seen, an opening bid can be made on as few as 12 points and even occasionally 11, but it could conceal considerably more. You would open 1 ♠ on all the following hands:

(a)	♠ AJ1073	(b)	♠ AQJ73	(c)	♠ AKQ73
	♡ J92		♡ J92		♡ J92
	◊ AQ32		◊ AQ32		◊ AK32
	♣ 7		♣ 7		♣ 7

As you can see, the point counts of these three hands differ considerably, from a minimum 12 in (a) through 14 in (b) to 17 in (c).

In fact, it is helpful to classify our opening bids as follows:

(11)	12-13	= Minimum
	14-15	= Above minimum
	16-17	= Good
	18-20	= Maximum

I have stopped at 20 because, with 21 points or more, you should use a stronger opening bid. These will be fully covered in the second book. For now, treat them as maximum opening bids and be grateful to hold such a wonderful hand.

As opener it is your task to make bids which show both your 'distribution' (i.e. the length of his suits) and your 'range', as described above. Your rebid continues that process.

Responder could have made two distinct types of bid i.e. limit or non-limit. We shall look at each in turn to see how it affects the development of the sequence.

Responder Makes a Limit Bid.

There are two variations here, either support for opener's suit or a no trump bid.

Over a supporting bid, our 'rules' are fairly easy:

1. *After a raise to the two level, e.g. 1♡-2♡*
   Opener should pass with a minimum or above minimum hand, suggest game by bidding at the three level with a good hand, and bid 4♡ with a maximum.

2. *After a raise to the three level, e.g. 1♡-3♡*
   Opener passes with a minimum hand and bids game otherwise.

3. *After a raise to four level e.g. 1♡- 4 ♡*
   Opener passes with all hands, except 'super maximums when slam could be bid – if you're brave enough!

After a 1NT response opener should describe his hand further. I will illustrate this with four examples. In all cases the bidding has started in the following way:

West	North	East	South
–	–	–	1♡
Pass	1NT	Pass	?

As South, you have to decide on your next action.

(a)	♠ Q107	(b)	♠ 7	(c)	♠ 7	(d)	♠ 63
	♡ KJ942		♡ KJ942		♡ KJ942		♡ KQ10842
	◇ AQ4		◇ AQ108		◇ AKQ8		◇ AQ4
	♣ Q9		♣ K93		♣ AJ3		♣ Q6

(a)
♠ Q107
♡ KJ942
◇ AQ4
♣ Q9

Recommended Bid: Pass

You have an above minimum hand, but remember that responder is limited to at most 9 points. With your 14 that makes you short of the requirements for game, even if facing a maximum hand.

You have no other suit to mention and with an essentially balanced hand and high cards in every suit, there is no reason to change the contract.

With stronger hands, you may be able to raise the level, e.g.

(i)
♠ Q107
♡ AKJ92
◇ AJ4
♣ Q9

Bid 2NT. 2NT asks responder to look at his hand and decide whether to gamble on a game contract. With six or seven points, responder would usually decline; with eight or nine accept.

(ii)
♠ AQ7
♡ AKJ92
◇ A104
♣ J9

Bid 3NT. With 19 points, you can guarantee enough combined strength to justify a shot at game. Nineteen plus a minimum of six gives you the magic '25'. No need to invite partner's co-operation, go straight to game.

(b)
♠ 7
♡ KJ942
◇ AQ108
♣ K93

Recommended Bid: 2◇

Partner does not have four spades, having chosen 1NT instead of 1♠. Hence the spade suit is a distinct weakness for no trump play. With healthy diamonds to bid, you have the answer. Partner can choose between playing in 2◇ or 2♡. With an equal number of cards in each, e.g.

♠ Q104
♡ Q73
◇ J94
♣ Q1082

Partner should always return to 2♡, because you will have at least as many cards in hearts and often, as here, more. Again, the partnership must strive to find the trump suit with the combined highest total of cards.

(c)

♠ 7
♡ KJ942
◇ AKQ8
♣ AJ3

Recommended Bid: 3◇

A 'jump' rebid showing a hand which is in the 'maximum' area. Adding our 18 points to partner's minimum of 6 suggests that we are close to game. *A jump re-bid in a new suit is forcing*, i.e. responder is obliged to make another bid; a pass is not permissible. This is because opener may be stronger still, say 19 or 20 points, and be investigating the most beneficial game contract. Even with a meagre six points, responder must make one more bid.

(d)

♠ 63
♡ KQ10842
◇ AQ4
♣ Q6

Recommended Bid: 2♡

Unlike the situation in (a), you can feel comfortable rebidding your six card heart suit. A 2♡ contract will give you security where 1NT will not. If you held a maximum or a good hand, you could act more strongly. For example:

(i) ♠ 63
     ♡ AQJ1084
     ◇ AQ4
     ♣ K6

     Bid 3♡

(ii) ♠ 6
     ♡ AQJ1094
     ◇ AQ5
     ♣ KQ6

     Bid 4♡

Responder Makes an 'Unlimited' Bid

This really means that responder could have a weak hand with as few as six points or a strong hand with as many as 15 points. Nearly all bids not covered in the last section are in this category.

Once more, opener's objectives are two-fold:

1. Continue to describe his shape.
2. Show extra strength when he has it.

Let us look at some examples. Imagine yourself to be South, deciding on your next bid:

West	North	East	South
–	–	–	1♡
Pass	2♣	Pass	?

(a) ♠ KJ3
♡ KJ1094
♢ KJ92
♣ 7

(b) ♠ AQ3
♡ AQ1094
♢ AQ92
♣ 72

(c) ♠ K3
♡ KJ982
♢ K6
♣ Q1082

(d) ♠ 76
♡ KJ10983
♢ AQ4
♣ Q6

(e) ♠ AJ4
♡ KJ973
♢ KJ9
♣ 72

(f) ♠ A6
♡ AJ1094
♢ 4
♣ A9542

Form your own view before reading on.

(a)
        ♠ KJ3
        ♡ KJ1094
        ♢ KJ92
        ♣ 7

Recommended Bid: 2♢

With a minimum hand, you simply continue to show your distribution. It is convenient that you did not have to raise the level, because otherwise a different problem may have arisen. Consider:

West	North	East	South
–	–	–	1♡
Pass	2◇	Pass	?

South holds:

♠ KJ3
♡ KJ1094
◇ 7
♣ KJ92

It would be unwise of South to bid 3♣ here, not because it fails to describe the hand, but because it raises the level to a nine-trick contract on a minimum hand. South should have at least an above-minimum and probably a good hand for such an action.

(b)   ♠ AQ3
                        ♡ AQ1094
                        ◇ AQ92
                        ♣ 7

Recommended Bid: 3◇

This is a jump rebid in a new suit and hence it is forcing. You can see that your 18 points, combined with partner's minimum of 9, gives your side enough for game. Therefore, you cannot allow North to pass below game level.

However, it is not clear *which* game to play so you need to explore the hand further before deciding on the final contract. Obviously you should have a better idea after North's reply.

(c)   ♠ K3
                        ♡ KJ982
                        ◇ K6
                        ♣ Q1082

Recommended Bid: 3♣

A raise of partner's suit to the minimum level suggesting minimum values. There is no requirement for partner to bid again.

(d)
    ♠ 76
    ♡ KJ10983
    ◇ AQ4
    ♣ Q6

Recommended Bid: 2♡

Rebidding your suit at the lowest available level suggests at most an above minimum hand. With a stronger hand, you would bid more. For example, with:

(i) ♠ K73
    ♡ AKJ1094
    ◇ 73
    ♣ A4

    Bid 3♡

(ii) ♠ K7
    ♡ AKJ10743
    ◇ A5
    ♣ J6

    Bid 4♡

You can always 'borrow' a point or two when holding a long suit with most of the top honours. I would consider hand (i) to be worth about 16-17 points and hand (ii) to be worth at least 18 points. Your jump bid has promised a good hand or better and has 'forced to game'. The bidding cannot then stop in a part-score.

(e)
    ♠ AJ4
    ♡ KJ973
    ◇ KJ9
    ♣ 72

Recommended Bid: 2NT

You could rebid 2♡, but a rebid in no trumps, suggesting stops in both spades and diamonds, describes the hand better.

(f)
    ♠ A6
    ♡ AJ1094
    ◇ 4
    ♣ A9542

Recommended Bid: 4♣

Although you hold a fairly minimum hand in terms of high cards, you have a wonderful fit for your partner's clubs and three aces. It is important that you stress this by giving jump support to show extra strength. It is not always the point count which determines the value of the hand.

Quiz on Rebids by Opener

Before we leave 'rebids by opener', here is a small test:

1. Why do some auctions last longer than others?

2. How many points do you need to have a 'good' opening bid?

3. What would you rebid, as South, in this position?

West	North	East	South
–	–	–	1♦
Pass	1♡	Pass	?

With:

(a)	♠ KJ94	(b)	♠ Q6	(c)	♠ KJ8	(d)	♠ AKJ4
	♡ K6		♡ AQ42		♡ Q		♡ 7
	◇ KQ1083		◇ AJ1083		◇ K10942		◇ AQJ103
	♣ Q7		♣ A6		♣ KQ103		♣ A73

4. What would you rebid, as South, in this position:

West	North	East	South
–	–	–	1♡
Pass	2♡	Pass	?

With:

(a)	♠ K104	(b)	♠ KJ7	(c)	♠ J	(d)	♠ AKJ
	♡ KQJ93		♡ KQ1094		♡ AQ1094		♡ Q98543
	◇ K1042		◇ KJ7		◇ AKJ95		◇ –
	♣ 7		♣ A6		♣ 65		♣ AQ94

Answers to Quiz on Rebids by Opener

1. Because a fit has not been found by the early bidding and there is sufficient strength held between the players to justify a continued search.

2. 16 or 17 (15 with a good six card suit).

3.

West	North	East	South
–	–	–	1♢
Pass	1♡	Pass	?

With:

(a) ♠ KJ94	(b) ♠ Q6	(c) ♠ KJ8	(d) ♠ AKJ4
♡ K6	♡ AQ42	♡ Q	♡ 7
♢ KQ1083	♢ AJ1083	♢ K10942	♢ AQJ103
♣ Q7	♣ A6	♣ KQ103	♣ A73
(a) 1♠	(b) 3♡	(c) 2♣	(d) 2♠

4. What would you rebid, as South, in this position:

West	North	East	South
–	–	–	1♡
Pass	2♡	Pass	?

With:

(a) ♠ K104	(b) ♠ KJ7	(c) ♠ J	(d) ♠ AKJ
♡ KQJ93	♡ KQ1094	♡ AQ1094	♡ Q98543
♢ K1042	♢ KJ7	♢ AKJ95	♢ –
♣ 7	♣ A6	♣ 65	♣ AQ94
(a) Pass	(b) 2NT (or 3♡)	(c) 3♢ *	(d) 4♡

* In example (c) the recommended bid of 3♢ does not suggest diamonds as trumps but rather describes the South hand and says that you hold a good hand, but not enough to bid game.

9
DEVELOPING THE AUCTION

Rebids by Responder

The auction is becoming lengthy. A rebid by responder is already the fourth bid of the sequence and may not terminate it (see next section). We need to develop a strategy that is clear cut, otherwise there is serious danger of not knowing what is going on.

I do not intend to cover every possible sequence which may occur, rather to look at certain types of sequences and draw general conclusions.

1. When opener rebids a new suit

The rebid of a new suit does not necessarily guarantee that the opener has a minimum hand, but does deny that he holds a good hand (where he would 'jump' rebid). Responder is allowed to pass at this stage, so as not to have to reach for the sky with two over extended hands.

Accordingly, any time responder has less than 10 points and a preference for the second suit, he should pass e.g.

West	North	East	South
–	–	–	1♡
Pass	1♠	Pass	2♢
Pass	?		

You are North, what do you bid with?

(a) ♠ KJ732	(b) ♠ KJ73	(c) ♠ KJ10873
♡ K6	♡ 86	♡ 7
♢ 95	♢ K53	♢ 74
♣ 9532	♣ Q532	♣ K753

My suggestions would be:

(a) 2♡. Remember that partner will always have at least as many hearts as diamonds. 2♡ is called 'simple preference' and does not suggest any extra strength.

(b) Pass.

(c) 2♠. With such poor support for both red suits, North is entitled to rebid the spades. Again the level is not raised, so no extra strength is implied.

With 'invitational' hands, i.e. those of sufficient strength that you wish to invite partner to bid game with an above minimum hand, you usually raise the level. After the same start of 1♡-1♠-2♢, as above, how would you proceed with these cards:

(a) ♠ A9753	(b) ♠ A9753	(c) ♠ AJ97
♡ KJ6	♡ K5	♡ 52
♢ K5	♢ KJ98	♢ K83
♣ 753	♣ 75	♣ K1075

I would bid as follows:

(a) 3♡. This is usually called jump preference (an interesting phrase indeed!).

(b) 3♢. With a weaker hand, e.g. without ♡K, you would pass 2♢, so to bid 3♢ suggests about this strength.

(c) 2NT. Showing about 11 or 12 points and a 'stop' (i.e. high cards and/or length) in the 'unbid suit' – in this case clubs. It tends to deny any real enthusiasm for openers' suits.

All these bids are not forcing, but they are encouraging the opener to proceed if he has anything to spare. With more strength, i.e. values sufficient to open the bidding, responder can go directly to game.

2. When opener makes a minimum rebid of his suit
The position is similar to (1) above in that responder can happily pass with up to 11 points, particularly so as the opener will often have a six card suit. Here are some examples:

West	North	East	South
–	–	–	1♡
Pass	1♠	Pass	2♡
Pass	?		

What would you bid, as North, holding the following cards:

(a) ♠ KJ543	(b) ♠ Q1073	(c) ♠ Q1073	(d) ♠ AJ10874
♡ 7	♡ Q73	♡ 73	♡ –
◇ KJ9	◇ KJ93	◇ KJ93	◇ Q732
♣ Q1073	♣ K7	♣ KQ7	♣ J73

My recommendations are:

(a) Pass. Not enough to bid 2NT and not good enough spades to bid them a second time. Partner's hearts should be good, so 2♡ is fine.

(b) 3♡. With 11 points, you can 'invite' South to bid game.

(c) 2NT. Also invitational but this time suggesting 3NT may be the best game contract.

(d) 2♠. You do not raise the level and you know that partner cannot have fewer cards in spades than you have in hearts! Little risk is involved in trying to improve the contract.

Again, none of these bids is forcing. Some invite game, whilst others suggest no extra values at all.

3. When opener raises your suit
In situations where a fit has already been established, your only decision is how high to go. You can parallel other sequences by saying that, if responder has fewer than 11 points, there is no reason to bid. With about 11 points responder can invite game, and with 12 or more go directly to game. Hence:

West	North	East	South
–	–	–	1♡
Pass	1♠	Pass	2♠
Pass	?		

(a) ♠ Q1073	(b) ♠ AQ1073	(c) ♠ Q10732
♡ Q107	♡ Q7	♡ Q7
◇ J94	◇ K93	◇ KJ93
♣ KJ7	♣ 987	♣ A7
Pass	Bid 3♠	Bid 4♠

4. When opener makes a jump rebid

Facing a maximum hand (18-20 points) it would be rare indeed not to play in game. Responder should judge which game he feels is best. For example:

West	North	East	South
–	–	–	1♡
Pass	1♠	Pass	3◊
Pass	?		

(a)	♠ AJ10983	(b)	♠ Q9832	(c)	♠ Q9832	(d)	♠ Q10732
	♡ 7		♡ 7		♡ 7		♡ Q98
	◊ Q43		◊ J43		◊ K43		◊ K7
	♣ Q73		♣ Q943		♣ Q1083		♣ J98
	Bid 4♠		Pass		Bid 3NT		Bid 4♡

Hand (b) is the exception to the rule, our occasional hand which can pass a 'forcing' bid. The others represent the normal choice of actions available to us.

Before we leave 'Responder's rebid', a brief test:

1.   When should responder raise the level of bidding?

2.   How many points are needed to 'invite' game?

3.   (a) What do you think South has shown in this sequence?

West	North	East	South
–	1◊	Pass	1♠
Pass	2♣	Pass	3♠
Pass	?		

(b) Is the 3♠ bid forcing?

Answers

1.   When he has an above minimum hand, usually at least 10 or 11 points.

2.   11 points or, occasionally, 10 with a good distribution.

3.   (a) Six card spade suit, enough to invite game, but not to bid it.
      (b) No, North should bid game with an 'above minimum' hand.

Ending the Sequence

Whilst it is crucial to know how to bid games and even slams, with confidence, it is just as important to realise when you should stop bidding. Nothing is worse than floundering around with no idea of whether you should still be bidding or could have passed a long time ago.

The key to the problem is being able to determine if partner's bid is forcing or not. If it is forcing, e.g. a jump bid, then the fact that you continued bidding means very little. If it is not forcing, any bid which raises the level shows extra strength. However, if you could have made a 'jump bid' yourself, then you too are limited if you choose a simple rebid, e.g.

West	North	East	South
–	–	–	1♡
Pass	1♠	Pass	2♣
Pass	2◇		

North's 2◇ shows diamonds and spades, but is limited by the failure to jump to 3◇ which would promise at least 12 points. Hence, South can pass 2◇. If, however, South now bids 3◇, he is showing an above minimum hand and is inviting game, but again, the bid is not forcing.

So, ending the sequence is not a difficult task, but beware of continuing to bid when you have a minimum hand and no fit. For example:

West	North	East	South
–	–	–	1♡
Pass	1♠	Pass	2♡
Pass	?		

You must pass, regardless of how much it hurts, with all the following hands:

(a) ♠ Q10732	(b) ♠ KJ98	(c) ♠ Q97532
♡ 7	♡ 7	♡ 73
◇ Q10732	◇ J109873	◇ K3
♣ Q6	♣ 74	♣ 732

The art of good bidding does not revolve exclusively around what to bid, although that is obviously vital; it also encompasses when to bid and when to pass.

We will develop strategy and increase sophistication later in the series. For now, we will **KISS** (Keep It Simple, Stupid)!

10
COMPETING THE BIDDING

When and How to Overcall

Sometimes you find that the side which opens the bidding has the minority of strength. Consider this pair of hands for example:

♠ J83
♡ 942
◇ J732
♣ J93

♠ 7
♡ J108
◇ AKQ108
♣ Q872

If South opens the bidding with 1◇, North with only 3 points will be forced to pass. South may or may not make 1◇; however, that is not the real issue on the deal.

As North/South have only 15 points between them, it means that East/West must have 25. That, as you saw earlier, should be enough for them to attempt a game contract. To do that, one of them must 'overcall'. Look at West's hand on the deal above.

West holds:

♠ AQ1094
♡ AQ73
◇ 64
♣ K10

West	North	East	South
–	–	–	1 ◊
?			

With a good opening bid of his own, West should not be afraid to enter the auction. The choice of action is much the same as for an opening bid, i.e. picking the longest suit. West should bid 1 ♠.

This has announced that the deal will be 'competitive' i.e. the two sides will compete for the right to play the contract. Much of the cut and thrust of bridge is contained within this area, with all the players jockeying their opponents around in an effort to get a plus score.

On this hand, the competitive element is hardly visible, because North is seriously out-gunned. West's intervention will force North to pass and East/West will take over. Maybe it would go something like this:

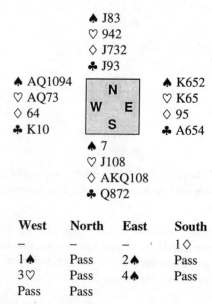

```
                    ♠ J83
                    ♡ 942
                    ◊ J732
                    ♣ J93
  ♠ AQ1094        ┌─────────┐        ♠ K652
  ♡ AQ73          │    N    │        ♡ K65
  ◊ 64            │  W   E  │        ◊ 95
  ♣ K10           │    S    │        ♣ A654
                  └─────────┘
                    ♠ 7
                    ♡ J108
                    ◊ AKQ108
                    ♣ Q872
```

West	North	East	South
–	–	–	1 ◊
1 ♠	Pass	2 ♠	Pass
3 ♡	Pass	4 ♠	Pass
Pass	Pass		

By bidding 3 ♡ West is asking partner to bid game with a maximum hand for the 2 ♠ raise and also helping his partner to make the right judgement by describing his hand further. This type of bid is often called a 'trial' bid and is ideal when you are mentally spinning a coin between playing in a part-score and chancing a game.

Sometimes, the competition is a little bloodier. Consider these four hands:

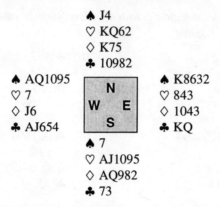

```
                    ♠ J4
                    ♡ KQ62
                    ◇ K75
                    ♣ 10982
    ♠ AQ1095                        ♠ K8632
    ♡ 7          ┌─────────┐        ♡ 843
    ◇ J6         │ W  N  E │        ◇ 1043
    ♣ AJ654      │    S    │        ♣ KQ
                 └─────────┘
                    ♠ 7
                    ♡ AJ1095
                    ◇ AQ982
                    ♣ 73
```

South opens the bidding and no one is vulnerable (which usually inspires great feats of heroism!). How do you think the bidding should proceed? Make your suggestion before reading on.

West	North	East	South
–	–	–	1♡
1♠	2♡	3♠	4♡
4♠	Pass	Pass	Pass

Never does bridge mirror the battle for an antique vase more than when both sides have around 20 points and each has a fit! Spice that up with a little extra distribution and combat commences.

Note how West, who might have opened 1♣ (see previous section on 'Opening Bids'), decides to overcall with 1♠. The reasons are:

(a) Spades outrank hearts, so in the fight for the contract East/West have a big edge. As you can see, North/South can make 4♡ (losing one spade and two club tricks), but it does them no good because they are out-bid *at the same level*. Had their opponents held a big fit in clubs, North/South would have been victorious, forcing their opponents to bid to the five level.

(b) The risk element is lower because West has only to make seven tricks in spades, compared with eight after an overcall of 2♣.

I will develop competitive bidding further later in this series but, for now, let us finish with our last Quiz:

Quiz on Competing the Bidding

1.   South opens the bidding with 1♡. Everyone is vulnerable, what do you bid as West, holding:

(a) ♠ AQ4
    ♡ K932
    ◇ Q
    ♣ J9432

(b) ♠ KJ7
    ♡ KJ8
    ◇ AQ43
    ♣ K106

(c) ♠ AKQ1094
    ♡ 7
    ◇ A43
    ♣ KJ7

(d) ♠ AJ1094
    ♡ K62
    ◇ Q104
    ♣ 73

2.   The bidding has proceeded as follows:

West	North	East	South
–	–	–	1♡
1♠	Pass	?	

No one is vulnerable, what do you bid as East with these hands?

(a) ♠ KQ3
    ♡ 743
    ◇ K932
    ♣ Q42

(b) ♠ J7
    ♡ Q1094
    ◇ AJ9
    ♣ KJ42

(c) ♠ 42
    ♡ J942
    ◇ AKQ106
    ♣ J4

(d) ♠ 4
    ♡ AQ1094
    ◇ J743
    ♣ J82

Answers to Quiz on Competing the Bidding

1. South opens the bidding with 1♡. Everyone is vulnerable, what do you bid as West, holding:

(a)
      ♠ AQ4
      ♡ K932
      ◊ Q
      ♣ J9432

Recommended Bid: Pass

Despite your 12 points, this hand has significant flaws. Your main suit is only jack high, you have a singleton honour which is bad, and you would have to bid at the two level. Caution should win the day.

(b)
      ♠ KJ7
      ♡ KJ8
      ◊ AQ43
      ♣ K106

Recommended Bid: 1NT

To overcall 1NT is riskier than opening it. This is because your opponents have already announced some strength. You would not consider bidding on a minimum opening therefore. I suggest you need at least 16 points to consider putting your head on the block. Note that the heart suit is well guarded with the K J being 'well-placed'. This is just another way of saying that you expect the ♡AQ to be on your right, thus giving you two tricks, rather than one.

(c)
      ♠ AKQ1094
      ♡ 7
      ◊ A43
      ♣ KJ7

Recommended Bid: 2♠

This is a 'jump' overcall, because you could have bid 1♠ instead. Hence you have voluntarily jumped a level. This type of bid should be reserved for hands of excellent playing strength with outstanding suits. Our example is an ideal candidate.

(d)　　　　　　　　♠ AJ1094
　　　　　　　　　　♡ K62
　　　　　　　　　　◇ Q104
　　　　　　　　　　♣ 73

Recommended Bid: 1♠

You would not open the bidding, but here it is permissible to make an overcall. The 'lower limit' for intervention is about 9 or 10 points with a good suit, if you can bid at the one level. Partner will not rely on a stronger hand than this.

The idea behind allowing a slightly wider and more flexible approach to intervening bids, is that you are able to compete more frequently. Otherwise, when the points are divided about equally, the opening side would almost always play the contract. By allowing more freedom to the other side, we get our 'auction'.

2. The bidding has proceeded as follows:

West	North	East	South
–	–	–	1♡
1♠	Pass	?	

No one is vulnerable, what do you bid as East with the following hands?

(a)　　　　　　　　♠ KQ3
　　　　　　　　　　♡ 743
　　　　　　　　　　◇ K932
　　　　　　　　　　♣ Q42

Recommended Bid: 2♠

With only three cards in spades, it is unusual to support straightaway. However, we must consider our alternatives. You cannot bid no trumps as you have no protection in hearts. You cannot bid a suit because diamonds, your only option, is a weedy four card specimen. You have too many points to pass. Thus you are left with 2♠.

Let us look at **1(d)** opposite **2(a)** and see if what you are doing is sensible.

♠ AJ1094		♠ KQ3
♡ K62	**N**	♡ 743
◇ Q104	**W E**	◇ K932
♣ 73	**S**	♣ Q42

Contract: 2♠ by West.

You can expect to lose at least two hearts, two clubs and one diamond, so our contract is a dicey one. If you hold your diamond losers to one, i.e. you successfully finesse against the jack, you will succeed. But then, both West and East have minimum hands, so that is about what you would anticipate.

Further North/South can probably make a contract of 2♣, so even if 2♠ fails, you will not have perished in vain!

(b)

♠ J7
♡ Q1094
◇ AJ9
♣ KJ42

Recommended Bid: 2NT

With a balanced 12 points, and stops in hearts, it is right to suggest game, and a jump response in no trumps is the best course of action. With a couple of points less, say:

♠ J7
♡ Q1094
◇ AJ9
♣ Q942

1NT would be sufficient and with a couple of points more, say:

♠ J7
♡ K1094
◇ AQ9
♣ KJ42

You would go to game immediately.

(c)
                              ♠ 42
                              ♡ J942
                              ◇ AKQ106
                              ♣ J4

Recommended Bid: 2◇

A good suit combined with 11 points makes raising the level perfectly sound. You do not know where you are going yet, but the journey will be interesting!!

(d)
                              ♠ 4
                              ♡ AQ1094
                              ◇ J743
                              ♣ J82

Recommended Bid: Pass

You should not bid 2♡ for two reasons:

(i)   You do not have enough points to raise the level.

(ii) Hearts have already been bid by South. The prospect of a double looms large on the horizon.

You could chance 1NT but, with poor 'stops' in the minors, that may not be any better than 1♠. Best to pass and look happy!

Conclusion

Well, not really a conclusion, more a summary of progress to date. I hope you have been absorbed by what you have discovered about bridge. There is much, much more and I intend to cover other aspects in the next two books.

I have still to examine card play technique in all its many guises and that will be the main thrust of the second book in the series. In addition, we will further develop our bidding strategy and look more closely at competition, at both high and low levels.

You have had the hors d'oeuvre. I trust you are now looking forward to the main course with relish. Please do not feel intimidated by the game, despite its, sometimes, unnecessary complexities.

It is worth conquering because your reward will be countless hours of entertainment and amusement in a social setting. And believe me, the sense of achievement in playing well is considerable.

I remember when I started playing golf, how pleased I was when I made a good shot. As I improved my mental attitude changed into being displeased with a bad one.

In bridge terms, you are in the former category, so go out and enjoy the game and look for the high spots.

The story continues ....